CALVARY AND SINAI;

Select Discourses,

ON

SUBJECTS OF ESSENTIAL IMPORTANCE.

INTENDED ESPECIALLY FOR THE FAMILY AND FRIENDS OF

THE AUTHOR.

BY J. COGSWELL, D. D.

WIPF & STOCK · Eugene, Oregon

Wipf and Stock Publishers
199 W 8th Ave, Suite 3
Eugene, OR 97401

Calvary and Sinai
Select Discourses on Subjects of Essential Importance
By Cogswell, J., D. D.
ISBN 13: 978-1-5326-8073-1
Publication date 1/30/2019
Previously published by A. Ackerman, 1852

INTRODUCTION.

The design of the author in sending these discourses to the press is not to offer them for sale, but to give an answer to those friends who know him, to the following supposed inquiry:

You have been more than forty years in the ministry—in the Pastoral Office twenty-three years, ten years Professor in a Theological Seminary, and to this day still in the ministry. While a pastor, several very interesting revivals of religion were experienced in your church and congregation, a good number were hopefully converted, some entered the ministry whose labors have been blessed, and some now occupy places of commanding influence. Your attention has daily been directed to the Holy Scriptures, and you have been exposed to the influences of almost every variety of opinion; now we ask, *On what ground are you willing* should rest your own hope of final salvation?

To those who make the above inquiry this volume is most affectionately dedicated by the AUTHOR.

SERMONS.

HOUSE OF GOD, CHRISTIAN'S BETTER HOME.

PSALM XXVII. 4.

"One thing have I desired of the Lord, that will I seek after, that I may dwell in the house of the Lord all the days of my life, that I may behold the beauty of the Lord, and inquire in his temple."

Thus the devout psalmist, when moved by the Holy Spirit, expressed his love of the house of God, and his desire to dwell in it all the days of his life. He valued the house of God more than the house in which he dwelt with his family. It was his resting-place, his better home. One day in seven spent in it afforded him more true happiness than the six spent in his own house. The Sabbath was his delight, holy of the Lord and honorable. "How amiable," he said, "are thy tabernacles, O Lord of Hosts! my soul longeth, yea, even fainteth, for the courts of the Lord: my heart and my flesh crieth out for the living God. Blessed are they that dwell in thy house, they will be still praising thee. For a day in thy courts is better than a thousand. I had rather be a door-keeper in the house of my God, than to dwell in the tents of wickedness." (Psalm lxxxiv.) He had rather occupy the humblest place in the house of God, than to be a royal guest in the tents of wickedness. He thought a day spent in the house of God a thousand times more precious than a day spent elsewhere.

The most costly feasts in the splendid habitations of the opulent, gave him no such entertainment as he enjoyed in the house of God.

His recollections of the house of God, when for a time excluded from it, awakened an intense desire of his return to it. "O God," he said, "thou art my God, early will I seek thee; my soul thirsteth for thee, my flesh longeth for thee in a dry and thirsty land, where no water is; to see thy power and thy glory so as I have seen thee in the sanctuary: because thy loving kindness is better than life, my lips shall praise thee." He could not forget the powerful impressions made on his mind in the house of God, when the Holy Spirit accompanied the different parts of public worship.

Similar were his feelings when he anticipated the return of the time for the worship of God in his house. "I was glad," he said, "when they said unto me, let us go into the house of the Lord, our feet shall stand within thy gates, O Jerusalem! Jerusalem is builded as a city that is compact together: whither the tribes go up, the tribes of the Lord, unto the testimony of Israel, to give thanks unto the name of the Lord." The worship of God seemed to dwell constantly on his mind. God was in all his thoughts. It was his earnest desire to do the will of God and glorify him in all his pursuits.

That he might make it manifest, not only to his people, but to all surrounding nations and to all succeeding generations, that his love of the true God was real and his thoughts of his character honorable, the king of Israel made preparations with an unsparing hand for the temple, which he was not allowed to build because he had been a bloody man, a man engaged in bloody wars. Not long before his death, when great riches were at his command, and which he had doubtless carefully kept for a sacred purpose, he said, "Now I have prepared with all my might for the house of my God, gold for things to be made of gold, and silver for things to be made of silver, and other things for other purposes, an immense amount of gold and silver." He gave freely for the house of God of his own proper good. He seemed to feel that he could not do too much to express his gratitude and love to God, who had done great things for him, and given him a good hope of an inheritance in heaven.

As the psalmist spake and acted as he was moved by the Holy Spirit; by his example we may form a correct opinion of our feelings toward God, whom we profess to love and worship.

It was the desire of the psalmist that his light should so shine before men, that they might see his good works and glorify his Father who is in heaven.

Now every christian has two homes—one where he dwells with his family, transacts business and manages his temporal affairs; the other where he attends to the concerns of his soul, and the things which relate to the kingdom of Christ. The latter is far more important than the former—as more important as his spiritual interests are more important than his temporal. The Christian feels that he has no home of very great value, if he have no place in the house of God, where he can enjoy the faithful ministry of the word, having none to molest him or to make him afraid. The home of the missionaries among the heathen is the house of God. Our pilgrim fathers and puritan ancestors felt that they had no home to which they desired to return, if they could have no house where they could worship God according to the dictates of their consciences. They left their country where they felt they had no home to leave, that they might find a place, a home in this western wilderness, where they could worship God according to their understanding of the scriptures. It was a house of God, and a home in it, which they desired, and for which they crossed the tempestuous ocean and submitted to severe privations and exposure to savage barbarity. In their conduct we see how much they valued for themselves and their families, a home in the house of God. The house of God cannot be a home to a Christian, if he is compelled to conform to a mode of worship, and liturgy, which his conscience disapproves in whole or even in part.

Some of the considerations will be mentioned, which make the house of God the most delightful home of the christian.

1. The house of God to which the text has reference was the tabernacle. The temple was built by Solomon, the son of David, king of Israel, and after the death of his father.

The tabernacle was a very costly and beautiful building. It was built according to a pattern God showed to Moses in the mount. So great was the liberality of the Hebrews in furnishing the various materials, of which the tabernacle was built that Moses was obliged to restrain them; for they brought much more than enough for the service of the work, which the Lord commanded to make. And Moses gave commandment, and they caused it to be proclaimed throughout the camp, saying, Let neither man nor woman make anymore work for the offering of the sanctuary. (Ex. xxxvi. 4, 6.) Women as well as men were equally concerned in furnishing materials and in working for the tabernacle, the first house ever built for the public worship of the true God. The temple built by Solomon, the most costly and splendid ever erected for the worship of God, was built according to a pattern God showed to David, the father of Solomon.

Should any inquiries be made, why were such costly and beautiful buildings erected for the worship of the great Jehovah? Does God delight in such things? Is not heaven his throne and the earth his footstool? Several answers may be given to such inquiries. It was the pleasure of God to try the feelings of the Hebrews toward him. He had delivered them from cruel bondage—supported them, and he gave them a perfect code of laws, more perfect, and far superior to any then known in the world. By building a tabernacle according to the pattern showed to Moses in the mount, the Hebrews gave visible proof of their gratitude to God—their honorable thoughts of his character, and their approbation of his laws. It was also the pleasure of God, that the Hebrews who came out of Egypt would make the impression on their posterity that their fathers loved and honored him, and felt their obligation to obey all his commands. The Hebrew nation, separated from all other nations, was the church of God, the light of the world. It was of great importance that parents should make the impression on the minds of their children, that they themselves loved and honored him, whom they required their children to obey and worship. When the rising generation saw the costly and beautiful house erected for the worship of God, they had visible proofs, better than mere professions, that their fathers highly respected him and thought him worthy of supreme love and adoration. No doubt when in Egypt they saw expensive temples, built for the worship of false gods. How then could it be manifest without some visible proof that the true God was as much loved and honored as were the gods of the Egyptians.

We know that the law of association has a powerful influence. In the worship of the true God, children should associate the ideas of beauty, order, convenience and excellence. How can Christians in dedicating a house to God for his worship express before the world honorable feelings toward him, unless they present an offering of real value? In the judgment of the world our offering would correspond with our feelings. Can we with right feelings present to God what is defective or mean? The following passage teaches us how God views those who offer to him what is of but little value. "And if ye offer the blind for sacrifice, is it not evil? and if ye offer the lame and sick, is it not evil? offer it now to thy Governor, will he be pleased with thee, or accept thy person? saith the Lord of hosts." (Mal. i. 8.) David would not worship God with that which cost him nothing. (2d Sam. xxiv. 24.)

Everything pertaining to the house of God should be, if possible, attractive, that the young may approach it with pleasure. The better home of the Christian, let it be remembered, is the house of God. He should give visible proof that he does view it as his better home,—that in which he most delights.

2. The house of God is the habitation where he dwells with his family, his adopted children, his sons and his daughters, all redeemed by the blood of his only begotten and dearly beloved Son. They are made heirs of God; "and if children," said the apostle, "then heirs, heirs of God, and joint-heirs with Christ, to an inheritance incorruptible and undefiled and that fadeth not away, reserved in heaven for them." (Rom. viii. 17.) God is always found at home in his house, when his people return to it. There he meets them, and by his Spirit communes with them. There he makes known his will—receives the worship of his people.

Though they may always enjoy his presence, "where two or three are met together in his name," yet the Sabbath is the day which God has more especially sanctified and blessed. On that day God always expects to see his children at home, unless prevented by some event of his providence, over which they have no control. No event of providence prevents God from meeting his people at the appointed time.

On the holy Sabbath, God speaks to his people by one whom he has called to be a saint and an ambassador. He calls men of like passions with their brethren, that they may listen to the word preached without fear, and may act understandingly and voluntarily in accepting the offers of mercy. This is the method God has adopted to publish his law to make known its extent and spirituality, its high claims on the sinner, and the impossibility of being justified by its deeds. No one can come to Christ and cordially receive him, till cut off from all dependence on the works of the law. "For I through the law," said the apostle, "am dead to the law, that I might live with God." (Gal. ii. 19.) To invite and to persuade sinners to come to Christ without showing them the justice of God in their condemnation, is only to encourage them to indulge a hope without any good foundation. Many, it is to be feared, without any better hope, have been encouraged to become members of the visible church. That preacher is unfaithful and unworthy of his office, who does not fearlessly assert and defend the claims of God. If faithful,

> "By him the violated law speaks out
> Its thunders; and by him in strains as sweet
> As angels use, the Gospel whispers peace."

The house of God is the place, where those called to be saints enter into a solemn covenant with him, and where the covenant is sealed and renewed from time to time by the ordinance of his appointment. Solemn is the scene and never to be forgotten when any enter into covenant with God, and in the presence of him that searcheth the heart, and in the presence of angels and men, and by their own act bind themselves to be faithful unto death.

3. As man is a social being, with strong social susceptibilities, God, who has a perfect knowledge of our nature and constitution, has made it our duty to worship him publicly. The appointment of one day in seven, which God has sanctified and blessed, was made that men might without any disturbance or interruption worship him. He only had the right to determine the time to be spent by the whole community in his house. Had no day been appointed by proper authority, his people would have been left in ignorance, and in a state of barbarity. In the places where the Sabbath is carefully observed we find the people more intelligent, more prosperous, more moral and religious, more enterprising and better supplied with the necessaries and comforts of life, than where the Sabbath with its privileges is neglected and profaned. Six days are sufficient to provide for all our temporal wants. Had not God himself appointed the day for public worship, on the same day one would be in his store, another in his office, another in his workshop and another in his field. It would be difficult for a whole community to agree on the day for the public worship of God. We see the wisdom and benevolence of God in the appointment of a day, and the very day and the portion of time to be spent in his service. His providence corresponds with his word. It has been found by innumerable proofs that those who rest one day in seven and spend it in the house of God, accomplish more than those who refuse or neglect to worship God on that day.

The public worship of God has many advantages. One man duly qualified is set apart and supported to minister in holy things—to declare, explain and defend the truths, to administer the Christian ordinances, and to attend to the proper government and discipline of the church.

Such is the nature of man, that the impressions made on his mind in a large assembly, is much more powerful than when he is in a very small circle. The heat we know is more intense where a *great fire* is raging, than it would be if the same combustibles were burning in a number of different places. Those, who meet in a large assembly mutually influence each other; they feel the power of sympathy; if one is awakened and converted, the change in the spirit and conduct of the individual is before every one. The inference drawn by many is that conversion is as necessary for them as it was for the subject of it. We find a variety in the dispositions and minds of a large assembly. As in the field of battle a few bold spirits lead, so in a religious assembly the timid and irresolute are willing to follow the more decided and zealous. The lovers of pleasure and amusement, when they would experience the highest degree of joy and delight, invite many to unite with them. The many in a large assembly strengthen in the few their belief in the truths taught.

The preacher, when he sees a large assembly before him, cannot but be more animated than when he sees before him but few, and his discourses not only make a deeper impression on the minds of his hearers, but produce more important results. There are some who feel as did Nicodemus, who went to Christ by night, unwilling to have it known lest the finger of scorn should be pointed at him, on account of his seriousness. But they are willing to meet with the multitude, because so many are found in the same place and are of the same opinion. The larger the assembly the greater its influence and the greater is the effect of the power of sympathy.

The establishment of a church in the world—the appointment of ordinances—the call of men to administer them as well as to preach the word, and oversee the conduct of all the members—to direct in the admission and discipline of the members, all have reference to public worship. We see the wisdom and benevolence of God in all the arrangements he has made for our benefit.

From the pulpit much important information may be communicated respecting the wants of the church in different parts of the world. Much land still remains to be possessed, and the church is constituted the light of the world, and it is made her duty to extend her light to all nations. "Go ye into all the world," said Christ, after his resurrection, to his apostles, "and preach the Gospel to every creature." They were commanded to "teach all nations, baptising them in the name of the Father and of the Son and of the Holy Ghost," teaching them to do whatever he commanded them; and to encourage them, he said, "Lo, I am with you always, even unto the end of the world. Amen." (Matt. xxviii. 19, 20.) Now the church must know what parts of the world are ignorant of the Gospel, or she cannot know her duty. Missionaries cannot go to the destitute without being sent by the church and being supported. The preacher is the proper person to make known the wants and duties of the church. This he can best do when the congregation is assembled.

When any enter the house of God, they see before them a man of like passions with themselves, by nature a child of wrath, but called of God and sent to them to offer to them free pardon on condition of their repentance and faith in his beloved Son, to point out to them the dangers to which they are exposed, and the way by which they may escape. The messages delivered, though delivered by a man, are really from God.

4. The house of God is the place where he more especially displays the power of his grace. The Holy Spirit operates with the word. The Scriptures were given by inspiration of God, and the Holy Spirit accompanies his own word, when faithfully exhibited. And the more clearly, solemnly and forcibly the truths of Christianity are exhibited, the more powerfully the Holy Spirit accompanies them. When those great truths, which have particular reference to that change essential to salvation, are fairly presented to the mind of the hearer, there seldom fails to be noticed a solemnity on the minds of the audience. No scenes on earth so deeply interest the Christian as those which pass before him in the house of God, when his work is revived by the powerful operations of the Holy Spirit. Then the church is quickened, refreshed, becomes prayerful and engaged in the cause of her Redeemer. Then sinners are awakened, convinced that they are justly condemned, and are heard to cry, "Men and brethren, what shall we do?" Then too, a greater or less number are hopefully converted—commence their lives anew, and rejoice in the hope of future happiness and glory. Then, too, important accessions are made to the church. Who can enter the house of God at such a time, and not be constrained to exclaim, "How dreadful is this place." The dependence of the church and the faithful preacher for success is not on the perfection of human instrumentality, but on the Spirit of God. "Unless the Lord build the house, they that build it labor in vain." It was in the taber-

nacle and in the temple where the glory of God appeared. It was in the holy city of Jerusalem where the Holy Spirit was poured out on the day of Pentecost, when three thousand were pricked in their hearts and were hopefully converted. The disciples, after the ascension of the Lord, spent ten days in prayer in an upper room in Jerusalem. In answer to their earnest prayers the Holy Spirit was poured out. This revival probably commenced in the upper room, where they had been assembled for prayer. Many times the power of the Holy Ghost has been felt in our churches. Such seasons are exceedingly desirable, and may be expected if we pray earnestly for them. Who can recollect such scenes without earnestly praying for a return of them. When God grants his church refreshing seasons, it appears to the hearer that God speaks to him—he hardly thinks of the person who addresses him. How affecting to the christian to see all around him, every one attentive to the preached word, to hear the sobbing of the awakened sinner, and to see the tear of joy sparkle in the eye of the new convert. The house of God, when his people are assembled, is the place and time where and when the power of his Spirit is felt.

5. The recollections of the house of God—of the scenes there witnessed and the feelings there experienced, are a perpetual source of satisfaction and happiness. What is heard with interest on the Sabbath is not forgotten during the week. New thoughts are suggested to the mind by the preacher, the remembrance of which is delightful. The discourse that was blessed to the conviction and conversion of the sinner he often calls to his remembrance. Many an hour is spent with pleasure by Christian friends in conversing on subjects discussed in the pulpit. "They that feared the Lord," said Malachi, "spake

one to another; and the Lord hearkened and heard it, and a book of remembrance was written before him for them that feared the Lord, and that thought upon his name." "By the rivers of Babylon," said the people of God in captivity, "there we sat down; yea, we wept when we remembered Zion. If I forget thee, O Jerusalem, let my right hand forget her cunning. If I do not remember thee, let my tongue cleave to the roof of my mouth; if I prefer not Jerusalem above my chief joy." The people of God could not forget, even when far away from their own country, the happy seasons enjoyed in the house of God. Seasons of holy communion at the table of the Lord are remembered with peculiar interest. Those who worthily partake of the Lord's supper, have the promise of enjoying a more excellent feast in the immediate presence of their Redeemer.

The house of God is the place where the mourner is comforted. If distressed on account of the loss of property or friends, the word of God applied to his mind by the Holy Spirit directs his thoughts to his heavenly inheritance, and to Christ, who is a friend which sticketh closer than a brother.

If mourning on account of his deficiencies in the performance of duty, the preacher directs his attention to the forgiving love of God and to the fullness there is in Christ. In the house of God the wanderer and backslider is reproved and shown the way by which he may return to God. The inquirer is taught how he may return to God—that the only way is through faith in Jesus Christ. Many careless and thoughtless sinners, who enter the house of God without any consciousness of their guilt, or any fear of future misery, receive impressions which terminate in that change which is essential to their salvation. Many too, who have entered the house of God in distress on account of their guilt, have, while attentively listening to the word preached, perceived the burden removed, the dark clouds which seemed to threaten their destruction broken and scattered, and the light of the glory of God, as manifested in his forgiving love, shining upon them. Who can describe the joy of the sinner, when he first indulges a good hope of salvation? The house of God is near to every one in this city. I speak not of any particular house of worship. There is variety enough to suit every one. It must be very disagreeable to a Christian parent, when he enters the house of God, to enter a crowd not knowing where to go—parents separated from their children, often husbands from their wives. But there are many who never treat their Creator and benefactor with sufficient respect to listen to his messages. God is no respecter of persons. The doors of his house are open to all who choose to enter, and to listen to the preaching of his word. To the poor as well as to the rich the Gospel is preached. They have an opportunity to secure for themselves an inheritance, infinitely more valuable than the greatest earthly possession, and it is offered *without money and without price.*

It appears from a review of this discourse that it is the duty of every Christian who is able to own a house, in which he dwells with his family, to own seats in the house of God for them. We know that every one who owns a house soon becomes attached to it, more than he can feel toward a hired house, or any public place, the occupancy of which is often changed. Every time the Christian approaches the house of God, he approaches his better home, and he should go to his own place in it with his family, assured that it is ready for him— the place ready consecrated by his prayers and tears, and by many interesting recollections.

What in the future world must be the reflections, how painful, how tormenting, of those whose lot by a kind providence was cast near some house of God where his word was faithfully preached, but which they seldom if ever entered? How must they feel when they see those whom they despised, while in the world, in their shining and glorified bodies, ready to possess the inheritance purchased for them, by Him in whom they trusted; while they themselves in their vile bodies are about to be cast into that flame where the worm dieth not and the fire is not quenched! This will be the view presented to all who make light of the preached word, and refuse to enter the house of God. If any cannot bear to hear these things now, how can they bear to feel them and to suffer the wrath of God forever? Come, for all things are ready, is now the invitation of Christ to every inquiring sinner; but at the great day, to all who refuse in time to accept it, he will say, "Depart, ye cursed, into everlasting fire, prepared for the devil and his angels." Amen.

GOD IS A SPIRIT.

JOHN IV. 24.

"God is a Spirit: and they that worship him must worship him in spirit and in truth."

THAT God is a Spirit, immaterial, invisible and omnipresent, infinite in power, wisdom and goodness, a God of truth, justice and mercy, has been the firm belief of all the truly pious of every age.

The worship of some god has been maintained almost universally by all mankind, by the most ignorant as well as by the most learned.

Man is a dependent and religious being. He feels his need of some superior power to deliver him from evils, which he cannot escape, and to grant him favors he cannot obtain, by his own exertions.

When originally created, man was like God, only infinitely inferior. He was able to discern and love the beauty and excellency of the divine character, and to do all that was required of him. So long as he continued innocent, he worshipped God in spirit and in truth.

But by his apostasy he became an enemy of God, could no longer discover anything lovely in the divine character, and could no longer delight in his service. Conscious of guilt, and impenitent, he sought to hide himself from his Creator. His descendants changed the "glory of the incorruptible God into an image made like to corruptible man, and to birds, and

Sermon on John iv. 24.

four-footed beasts and creeping things. They changed the truth of God into a lie, and worshiped and served the creature more than the Creator, who is blessed forever. Amen." (Rom. i. 23, 25.)

By far the greatest part of mankind are now ignorant of the true God, and are the worshipers of idols. "Their idols are silver and gold, the work of men's hands. They have mouths, but they speak not; eyes have they, but they see not; they have ears, but they hear not; noses have they, but they smell not; they have hands, but they handle not; feet have they, but they walk not; neither speak they through their throats. They that make them are like them; so is every one that trusteth in them." (Psalm cxv. 4—8.)

Though we cannot see God, who is an invisible Spirit; yet we may know him from His works and word. "For the invisible things of Him from the creation of the world, are clearly seen, being understood by the things that are made, even his eternal power and Godhead; so that they (idolaters) are without excuse." (Rom. i. 20.)

Since mankind are disposed to worship some god, and since by their apostacy, they have lost their knowledge of the true God; where the light of revelation is not enjoyed, they worship visible gods. Feeling the necessity of a present god, and ignorant of Him who is an omnipresent Spirit, they so multiplied their gods as to have one present in every place and for every occasion. Though they acknowledge, without being aware of it, the necessity of an omnipresent Spirit, infinite in power, wisdom and goodness. They know that a material, visible god can be in but one place at one time. To supply this deficiency they have made many gods.

In those countries which are nominally Christian, but where

the people are not allowed the free use of the Scriptures, we find them ignorant of the nature of that worship, which God, who is a Spirit, can accept.

All attempted visible representation of God, of Christ, or of the prophets, apostles or martyrs, can give us no correct knowledge of their characters. The external appearance of some of the vilest persons that have ever lived, has been beautiful. Uncommon excellence of character has sometimes been found in a deformed body. Christ, when on earth, was "a man of sorrows and acquainted with grief;" "His visage was so marred more than any man, and his form more than the sons of men." (Is. lii. 14.) When revealed to the Christian by the Spirit, he appears to be "the chief among ten thousand, and altogether lovely." The pictures seen in some churches are deceptive. They cannot give a true knowledge of the characters of the persons they are designed to represent. They encourage a spirit of idolatry. The thoughts of the worshipers rest on the pictures, and never reach to God, who is a Spirit. The deceptive impression made by a beautiful picture is lasting. It cannot be excluded from the mind.

Why does the devout Christian, when he most deeply feels the need of Divine aid, and would most earnestly plead with God for help, retire to his closet, shut the door and close his eyes, that nothing visible may prevent him from worshiping God, who is a Spirit, "in spirit and in truth?" And why do the most pious and successful pastors of our churches, when offering prayer to God in the sanctuary for a blessing on the people committed to their charge, close their eyes? Do they not close their eyes that nothing may disturb their intercourse and communion with Him, who is an invisible spirit, and whom they desire to worship with the inmost feelings of their hearts?

The character given to the idols worshiped in all pagan nations corresponds with their corrupt desires and practices. External and visible forms and rites, if they satisfy the professed friends of God, ruin their souls.

II. "They that worship God, must worship him in spirit and in truth."

1. They must worship him *in spirit*.

To worship him in spirit is to worship him with the inmost feelings of the heart. There must be no reserve. When any are born of the Spirit, the deep feelings of their heart flow out to God. There is a wide difference between the worship of a real Christian, and one whose heart has never been renewed, however orthodox he may be, and however serious he may be when in the pulpit. Man looketh on the outward appearance, but God looketh on the heart. He is worthy of our supreme love. There is no defect in his character. It is infinitely excellent, perfect and glorious.

When the light of the glory of God's forgiving love first breaks in upon the mind of a sinner, who has been a subject of deep conviction, he forgets himself, and the deep affections of his heart flow out to the object which engages all his thoughts, and completely fills his soul. False hopes, by which sinners, who have been alarmed, are delivered from their fear of future punishment, may move their feelings. Their hearts may overflow with love to Him, who has done so much for them. But their love may be selfish. They do not love God on account of the excellency of his character, but on account of his supposed goodness to them. The worship of such persons is selfish, deceptive and ruinous. Their whole concern is to escape deserved punishment, and to obtain happiness. They manifest no concern for the honor and glory of God.

There seems to be a foundation for the three-fold distinction, noticed by the apostle in the following passage (1 Thess. v. 23): "And the very God of peace sanctify you wholly, and I pray God your whole spirit, and soul and body be preserved blameless unto the coming of our Lord Jesus Christ."

The Scriptures in various passages, notice a distinction between the spirit of a man, and the affections of his heart. "The sacrifices of God are a broken spirit; a broken and a contrite heart, O God, thou wilt not despise." (Psalm li. 17.) "The Lord is nigh unto them that are of a broken heart, and saveth such as be of a contrite spirit." (Psalm xxxiv. 18.) "For thus saith the high and lofty One, that inhabiteth eternity, whose name is holy; I dwell in the high and holy place, with him also that is of a contrite and humble spirit, to revive the spirit of the humble, and to revive the heart of the contrite ones." (Isaiah lvii. 15.)

The spirit of man is the governing principle of his soul. This determines his character. We often speak of a bold, a timid and an angry spirit; but do not use these expressions when speaking of the heart. A humble and contrite spirit is the spirit of a sincere christian.

Now there is in every true christian that which is born of the Spirit of God. This is holy, and all its powers are holy. No unholy thought ever *originates* in that which is born of the Holy Spirit. Though constantly opposed by the spirit of the old man, yet it always gains the victory, and always increases in power. It is this which makes a man a subject of the kingdom of Christ, and entitles him to all the privileges and blessings promised to the children of God. The christian is no longer a subject of the kingdom of the god of this world. This was doubtless the understanding of the apostle, when he thus expressed himself: "For that which I do, I allow not, for what I would, that do I not; but what I hate, that do I. If then I do that which I would not, I consent unto the law that it is good. Now, then, it is no more I (the christian) that do it, but sin that dwelleth in me." (Rom. vii. 15—17.) While the christian is in the present state, there is a constant warfare between the spirit of the old man and the spirit of the new man. The spirit of the latter is at first feeble, and though many times overcome by superior powers, yet by the promised help of the Holy Spirit, is always finally victorious. The trials through which the christian is called to pass, enable him to discover the remains of depravity in his heart, and the sanctifying influences of the Holy Spirit help him to mortify the deeds of the body. The death of the body ends the warfare. When the apostle prayed that the God of peace would sanctify the whole spirit, his meaning, doubtless, was, that the spirit of the old man might be subject to the spirit of the new man, so that the spirit of the latter might act freely and without any hindrance. He knew that the affections of the heart would correspond with the spirit—indeed, that all the powers of the soul would be subject to its control. It was also his prayer that the powers of the body might be so employed as best to answer the design of their Creator. In the performance of our duty, much depends on the strength of our body. Any habit or practice which impairs the strength of the body, is sinful. It robs God of the service he justly requires of us.

The sanctification of the whole spirit, soul and body, produces that peace which passeth understanding, and which is an earnest of that peace which will be everlasting.

Now, there are seasons in the experience of the pious, when the new man is victorious, and all his powers are subject to the law of Christ. When the Holy Spirit "bears witness with their spirits that they are the children of God," then their doubts are scattered—then their warmest affections flow out to their Redeemer, whose glory is revealed to them by the Holy Spirit, then the worship of God is a delight.

To promote the work of sanctification in the hearts of christians, God makes use of the preaching of his word, and of the events of his providence. He takes from them those objects on which their affections are too strongly placed. He takes from the covetous man his property—from a too indulgent parent a beloved child. In various ways God meets those who are beginning to go astray, and sends them weeping back to the path of duty. Hypocrites are often left in this world to expose their hypocrisy. "And we know that all things work together for good to them that love God, to them who are called according to his purpose." (Rom. viii. 28.) All the trials of the christian, when sanctified, deepen his repentance, increase his love of God, strengthen his faith, humble his pride, weaken his attachment to worldly possessions and brighten his hope of an inheritance, "incorruptible, undefiled, and that fadeth not away."

2. They that worship him must worship him *in truth.*

Our Divine Lord, not long before he left the world, offered to his Father the following prayer for his disciples: "Sanctify them through thy truth; thy word is truth." (John xvii. 17.) He knew that if they received the essential truths of the Gospel in the love of them, that they would never so fall away as to perish. The promise of God would sustain them in all their trials. His prayer was, that the work of sanctification should extend to all the truths of the Gospel, which they would be most tempted to reject or modify. The truth, when sanctified, never appears more glorious than when contemplated in its simplicity. In the works of the most pious, who have passed through the most fiery trials, we find the clearest exhibitions of those truths, to which the unrenewed are most opposed.

1. To worship God in truth, is to worship him according to the revelations made of himself, and of the plan he has devised and adopted for our redemption.

The revelations God has made of himself and of the method he has adopted for the salvation of sinners, must correspond with truthful realities; and it must be highly offensive to God to maintain that any of his revelations are unnecessary or unimportant. The character of a well educated and mature christian, if correctly described, would be found to correspond with all the teachings of the volume of revelation. Those doctrines and precepts which have reference to christian experience, are found to be written in the heart, and established in the life of every one that has been born of the Holy Spirit. We have no right to reject or modify any truth we find in the volume of revelation.

It is a remarkable fact that some unable to read, and others who have no book but the Bible, but who have been born of the Holy Spirit, when giving an account of the change wrought in them, admit without hesitation, those doctrines, concerning which the learned have always disputed. They give a correct account of their convictions, their discovery of the deep depravity of their hearts, the great change wrought in them by the Holy Ghost, and their views of the glory of God shining in the face of Jesus Christ. When they hear the truths of revelation clearly exhibited in their simplicity, they find a response in their hearts. Unless the change wrought in us corresponds with the teaching of the inspired volume, our hope of salvation must be of no value. If we feel an opposition to any of the doctrines of Scripture, especially the doctrines of christianity, we have reason to be alarmed, and to fear that we have never been renewed by the Holy Spirit. But, we sometimes find persons *apparently* opposed to certain doctrines of Scripture, when in fact they are only opposed to caricatures of them, given by those in heart really opposed to them. One of the methods adopted by the enemies of the truth to destroy its influence, is to caricature the most essential doctrines of grace, that they may appear unreasonable and unworthy of notice.

How can we worship God *in truth* unless we have a correct view of our guilt and unworthiness by nature—a sense of obligation to him for his distinguishing grace? If we persuade ourselves that we have by our own efforts effected our salvation, or made ourselves to differ, we rob God of his glory, and despise those no worse by nature than ourselves. Why God takes this person and passes by that, we know not. In the same family where all enjoy the same privileges, we often see one taken and another left. God has a perfect right to bestow his favors as he pleases. He is under no obligation to save any of the human race, for all are sinners, and condemned by that law, which is holy and just and good. We have reason to rejoice that he is willing to save any who sincerely repent of their sins and believe in the Lord Jesus Christ. The condition of men in this world is determined by the providence of God. Why one becomes rich, and another continues poor, we know not. One is not made rich because he is better than his poor neighbor, nor because he makes greater efforts to increase his substance than his poor neighbor. It is in vain to contend against God, and it is folly to disregard the evidence of our senses. None but those who have been born of the Holy Spirit can cordially approve the distinguishing doctrines of grace. The Scriptures teach us that "the carnal mind is enmity against God, is not subject to his law, neither indeed can be." (Rom. viii. 7.) Its enmity is more especially manifested against the doctrines of christianity, because Christ is the brightness of his Father's glory and the express image of his person. The doctrines of the cross try the feelings of the human heart.

There are some who are ready to express their approbation of the moral law, which is the law of nature, but who reject the peculiar doctrines of grace. Some favor the second table of the law, who neglect the first table. The works of creation declare the unity of God, but give us no knowledge of a plurality of persons in the godhead, and no knowledge of the method God has devised and adopted for the redemption of men. The Scriptures more clearly than the works of nature declare the unity of God. We are indebted to them for all we know of any way by which we can be saved. Many are unwilling to receive doctrines, to which their unrenewed hearts are opposed, on the testimony of God. Though not the worshipers of idols, which are visible, they worship gods, which are the creatures of their imagination, or the offspring of their reason. From a survey of the works of nature, or from their knowledge of physical laws they form their ideas of what God is, or ought to be, to be worshiped by them. Others, who profess to believe the Scriptures, knowing the feelings of the wealthy and the learned toward the humbling doctrines of the gospel, have endeavored to modify those doctrines, to which the unrenewed are most opposed, by some philosophical theory. In this way the church has been from age to age corrupted. The most faithful servants of God have in many instances been driven from the heights of Zion to establish churches among the destitute. The most faithful and successful pastors, who, at the close of life have left large and wealthy congregations have, in not a few instances, been succeeded by ambitious and popular preachers, who have cared more for their own interest than for the salvation of their people.

The doctrines of christianity, if carefully examined, must appear reasonable. No one will deny that he is a sinner, a transgressor of that law, which is holy, just, and good. And it must be evident that the law of God must be executed, or his government cannot be respected. He has declared that the soul that sinneth shall die. The veracity of God demands the execution of His law. Should any be pardoned without an atonement, how must God appear to the angels that sinned, who were banished from Heaven, and are reserved in chains and darkness unto the judgment of the great day; and how must God appear to holy angels, who saw their companions punished without any offer of pardon? God must manifest consistency of character, or he cannot be worshiped. Now the Son of God has become a substitute, approved by his Father for all who will trust in Him. He has assumed our nature, and united it with the Divine nature. Thus two natures mysteriously are united in one person. This person has magnified the Divine law and made it honorable by his obedience and death. This Divine nature has given an infinite value to what he has done. Mercy and truth have met together in Him, and righteousness and peace have kissed each other. By His resurrection from the dead, God the Father has given proof that He is fully satisfied with the part performed by His beloved Son, our substitute.

Now, whether we fully understand or not the plan God has adopted for our salvation, we have the united testimony of all true Christians, that as soon as they came to Christ by repentance and faith they were made happy ; and their happiness far exceeded any they had ever before experienced. In addition to this they had a firm hope, such as they never had before, of immortal life and glory. Ought not their testimony to be received ? They declare what they have seen and felt, and their testimony is counteracted or contradicted only by the testimony of those who never experienced what they have. In a court of justice are witnesses who have not seen, and do not know, only from report, to be compared with those who have themselves seen, and can relate all the circumstances. The testimony of feeling is as strong as sight. Besides, we have the testimony confirmed by many years' experience, many times tried, as by the most searching cross-examination. Let me give you the testimony of one witness. " I was, like many others, occupied with worldly pursuits ; but the word of God was applied to my conscience, and I felt that I was a condemned sinner—justly condemned. I found that my heart was hard, opposed to the holy character of God, and that I must perish without a new heart. In my distress, I looked to Christ as the only Saviour, and when my thoughts were fixed on Him, I perceived a change in my heart. Light burst in upon my mind. Christ appeared to be the ' chief among ten thousand, and altogether lovely ;' my hard heart became tender, and my affections flowed out to Him ; the glory of God appeared in His word and works. Old things were passed away, and all things became new. The change became permanent, and has so continued for many years. I now have a prevailing hope that death will only be the door through which I shall enter the world of happiness and glory."

APPLICATION.

1. Since God is an Omniscient and Omnipresent Spirit, we know that He is always near us by night and by day, when we go out and come in; that He has a perfect knowledge of all our wants, our conduct, and our temptations; that He is ready to hear our prayers, and is able and willing to grant us what we need. This consideration is a source of great comfort to all sincere Christians. Great are the privileges of those who are in covenant with God, and who, in all their trials, have an Almighty friend near them to deliver them from dangers seen and unseen. The covenant God has established with His people abounds with promises, corresponding with all their real wants. He will never leave nor forsake any who trust in Him. But it is a fearful thing for the sinner, unrenewed, to be always in the presence of a holy God, whose all-piercing eye is ever upon him, and who has a perfect knowledge of all his thoughts. This should make him afraid to offend God, who is angry with the wicked, and should make him anxious to be reconciled to Him.

2. As God requires those who worship Him to worship Him in spirit and in truth, they ought not to be satisfied with their hope of future happiness, unless they have good evidence that they worship God according to the revelations He has given of Himself, and the plan He has adopted for our redemption, and with the inmost feelings of our heart. All mere outward service is an offence to God, if the heart is withholden from

Him. The Christian is never so happy as when the deep feelings of his heart flow out to God. Men of the world discern a difference between prayers, which proceed from the heart, and such as are formal. When we worship God in spirit, His spirit witnesseth with our spirit that we are the children of God. It is to be feared that many, who are members of the visible church, have never experienced that deep work of grace in their hearts which fitted them to worship God in spirit. They seem to be satisfied, if they manifest external respect for the institutions of Christianity. Their prayers may be the prayers of men of doubtful piety, who lived centuries before they were born. The prayers offered to God ought surely to express the feelings we have *at the time they are offered*. That religion which secures the salvation of the soul must be personal. We must ourselves repent, believe, and worship God in spirit and in truth, or we cannot reasonably hope for salvation. It is the highest happiness of the real Christian himself to commune with God.

Finally, remember, my brethren, God has assured us that the unsanctified heart is enmity against Him, and that it is deceitful above all things, and desperately wicked; and as men feel the necessity of some religion, they are disposed to embrace that which requires the least self-denial, and which will give peace to their minds. Now, let me ask, can a saving change be wrought in a heart naturally at enmity against God, unless doctrines are received, to which the unrenewed heart is opposed? If men only hear those doctrines which are agreeable to their natural feelings, and which are highly approved by men of the world, they cannot experience that change, without which they cannot be saved. Does not the true convert love those truths he once opposed—and love those duties he once disliked? The change is in him, not in the word of God. The spirit of God operates with those truths, which wound the feelings of the unrenewed, and makes them effectual to their salvation. Those who preach so as to please men of the world, and to be admired by them, have no reason to expect that their hearers will be truly converted. They may fill their churches, and be liberally supported; but fearful will be the account which they must render to Him who is appointed to judge the world.

Those who minister in holy things, must exhibit clearly and affectionately the mind of the Spirit, the author of the inspired volume; and those who would make sure of salvation, must never be satisfied till their hearts are reconciled to all the doctrines and precepts of revelation, and they can receive, without reserve, Christ in all his offices, as their glorious Redeemer. AMEN.

THE HOLINESS OF GOD.

ISAIAH VI. 1—3.

"In the year that King Uzziah died, I saw also the Lord sitting upon a throne high and lifted up, and his train filled the temple.

"Above it stood the Seraphims: each one had six wings; with twain he covered his face, and with twain he covered his feet, and with twain he did fly.

"And one cried to another and said, Holy, holy, holy is the Lord of Hosts, the whole earth is full of his glory."

The death of Uzziah, who was fifty-two years king of Judah, was not in itself an event of much importance, only as it determined the year when the prophet Isaiah had the remarkable vision, which the text in part describes. Till he became a leper he was an able statesman, a mighty warrior, and a renowned sovereign. As long as he sought the Lord, God made him to prosper. But when he was strong, his heart was lifted up to his destruction. Because he transgressed against the Lord his God, and went into the temple of the Lord to burn incense, which none but the priests were allowed to perform, he became a leper, and continued to be thus punished till the day of his death.

Though the worship of the true God during the reign of Uzziah was outwardly maintained, yet it was greatly corrupted by the idolatrous practices which were tolerated. The wickedness of the professed friends of God provoked Him to anger against them. To prepare the prophet Isaiah, whom he sent to instruct and reprove them, to meet the opposition to which he would be exposed, and the cruel persecution he would suffer, God was pleased to make him more perfectly acquainted with his holy character and purposes concerning the people, among whom he was called to labor. In like manner our Divine Lord and Master, not long before his crucifixion, knowing what treatment his disciples would receive from this wicked world, thus addressed them: "If the world hate you, ye know that it hated me before it hated you. If ye were of the world, the world would love his own; but because ye are not of the world, but I have chosen you out of the world, therefore the world hateth you. Remember the word that I said unto you, The servant is not greater than his master. If they have persecuted me they will also persecute you; if they have kept my saying, they will keep yours also. All these things will they do unto you for my name's sake, because they know not him that sent me." (John xv. 18—21.)

The vision Isaiah had of the holiness of God, was suited to prepare him for the very difficult work assigned him. It deeply affected him, and gave him the most abasing view of himself. Thus he expressed his feelings: "Then said I, Wo is me! for I am undone; because I am a man of unclean lips, and I dwell in the midst of a people of unclean lips; for mine eyes have seen the King, the Lord of Hosts."

The person whom Isaiah saw seated on a throne high and lifted up, is the Son of God, our mediatorial King. Of this we have proof in the 12th chapter of the Gospel of John. The Evangelist, after noticing the miracles of Christ, and the unbelief of the Jews, adds: "These things said Esaias, when he saw His glory and spake of him." (John xii. 40.)

The throne, "high and lifted up," on which the prophet saw the Son of God sitting, may intimate that the work of Redemption is a more glorious exhibition than the work of creation, of

Sermon on Isaiah vi. 1–3.

the holy character of God. The former was, doubtless, that on which the mind of our Divine Lord was fixed.

The Son of God appeared in the temple, which had been greatly polluted, to consecrate it anew. During his ministry on the earth, he drove from his Father's house those that sold oxen and sheep and doves, and the changers of money.

"Above the throne stood the Seraphims." These are supposed to be the highest order of angels. They dwell near the throne of God, and never cease to worship him with all their powers. They are ministering spirits to Christ and to his church. The work of redemption is that which interests them deeply, and into which they desire to look.

"Each one had six wings; with twain he covered his face." This may intimate that they were unable to bear a full view of the dazzling splendor of the glory of the holiness of God shining in the face of his beloved and only begotten Son. God would not permit Moses, distinguished as he was for piety, to behold his face. He said to him, "Thou canst not see my face; for there shall no man see me and live." In mercy, God makes only such revelations of his perfections to men as they are able to bear.

"With twain each of the Seraphims covered his feet." This may intimate that the highest order of angels feel that their very best services are unworthy of the notice of Him who is infinitely holy. The more distinguished any christian is for piety, the less he thinks of what he has done for Him who gave his life to redeem him. Well might the Seraphim view the greatest work they ever performed, of small importance compared with what the Son of God undertook and has accomplished for our redemption. When their thoughts were directed to God, their knowledge compared with his, appeared to be but ignorance—their wisdom but folly—their strength but weakness, and their holiness but an obscure reflection of the holiness of their Creator. How circumscribed must be the views of all finite beings, even the most intelligent, and how limited the range of their noblest thoughts! "For my thoughts are not your thoughts, saith the Lord, neither are your ways my ways. For as the heavens are higher than the earth, so are my ways higher than your ways, and my thoughts than your thoughts."

"With twain each of the Seraphims did fly." This may signify their readiness to obey the commands of God, and the celerity with which they executed them. The greater the advancement of any christian in holiness, the more ready he is to do the will of God, however difficult the duty he is called to perform, and the more rapid and energetic his movements in the accomplishment of the object of his pursuit.

This view of the Seraphim is a beautiful representation of the humility and obedience of holy angels in heaven. It may, however, be observed, the humility of *holy angels* is in some respects different from that of christians. The former cannot be conscious of guilt, and consequently cannot repent and experience brokenness of spirit and contrition of heart. They never feel forgiving love, but when they behold the glory of the holiness of God, they have a deep sense of their unworthiness of his notice. "The heavens are not clean in his sight and his angels he chargeth with folly." The infidel may be convinced that he is infinitely inferior to God in knowledge, wisdom and power; but may be unwilling to confess his guilt, or to look to Christ for pardon. Ignorant of the holiness of God, he has no sense of his vileness.

While the thoughts of the Seraphims were fixed on him

whom they saw sitting on a throne high and lifted up, and also, doubtless, on the plan and work of Redemption, they cried one to another, and said, "Holy, holy, holy is the Lord of Hosts, the whole earth is full of his glory."

No discourse was delivered by any one of them—no hymn was sung, but the single word "*holy*" seemed to comprehend and express their thoughts of the glory of God's holiness, as it shone in the face of Him that sat upon the throne high and lifted up. Whether the pronouncing of the word "holy" three times by the Seraphims be any evidence of their adoration of three persons in the ever blessed Trinity, we cannot certainly determine. That they had a knowledge of a plurality of persons in the Godhead cannot be questioned. " The secret of the Lord is with them that fear Him." God appeared to them to be holy in all the revelations he had made of himself, in his works of creation, providence and redemption. *The moral law* is a transcript of his character as made known to our first parents before their apostasy. This law is holy, just and good. *The law of faith* is a transcript of the Divine character, as made known to man after his apostasy. This cannot be understood without a knowledge of the doctrine of the Trinity. This law is holy and just and merciful, as well as good. There can be no doubt that the Seraphims had a correct understanding of the revelations which God had made of his gracious purposes concerning perishing men. These revelations became more full and particular, till the christian church was firmly established in the world.

The holiness of God is that perfection of His character, on which the Seraphims delighted to dwell. This seemed to be the all-absorbing subject of their meditations. This very important and sublime subject we ought to understand. For "without holiness no man shall see the Lord."

This is the subject to which your attention is now directed. It may be observed,

1. Freedom from moral evil, a common definition of the holiness of God, is by no means a satisfactory view of this perfection.

Freedom from moral evil may be predicated of beings not capable of sinning. There can be no moral evil in any of the lower orders of animals. They are not subjects of the moral government of God. They have no discernment of the difference between good and evil in a moral sense.

That God was as holy as he is now before he created any of the subjects of his moral government, and consequently before moral evil existed, is evident from the consideration of his immutability. It may here be added, destitute of holiness is not a satisfactory view of human depravity. To be destitute of that holiness which God requires of men, is not necessarily to be depraved. The lower orders of animals are not depraved, though destitute of that holiness which is essential to the christian character. It is true, the subjects of God's moral government, who are destitute of holiness, are depraved, and totally depraved.

2. The holiness of God does not consist *merely* in his hatred of sin.

God does indeed hate sin, and looks upon all transgressions of his moral law with abhorrence. Hatred of sin where it exists and is known, is essential to holiness of character, and the greater the advancement of any in holiness, the greater is their hatred of sin. God, who is infinitely holy, looks upon all sin with infinite abhorrence. But the holiness of God was clearly manifested in heaven before the apostasy of the angels that sinned, and consequently before he could exercise hatred of sin. This holiness did not depend for its existence or manifestation on the transgression of his law.

3. It appears to be a very common opinion that the holiness of God has respect only to the subjects of his moral government. That they hold the highest place in his thoughts and affections, is readily admitted. Man is constituted the lord of this lower world. "He was made but little lower than the angels, and crowned with glory and honor." The government of the world has always had respect to his moral conduct. The history of the Jews affords abundant proofs of the correctness of this observation. The course of Divine providence corresponds with their conduct. When faithful in the performance of religious duties, they were prosperous; but when they departed from God he visited them with his judgments. Many are the works of God in which moral beings appear to have no immediate interest, and which have no moral character. The moral kingdom of God embraces but a small portion of his creatures, and occupies but a small space in his vast empire. But the government of God is universal in extent, and everlasting in duration. "Not a sparrow falleth to the ground without him, and the very hairs of our head are all numbered." This holiness extends to all his works.

4. The holiness of God is essential to his nature and character. "This," observes a distinguished divine, "is the blessedness and nobleness of his nature; it renders him glorious in himself, and glorious to his creatures, that understand anything of this lovely perfection. The holiness of God is his glory and crown." "Who is like unto thee," sang Moses and the children of Israel, when they had crossed the Red Sea, "glorious in holiness, fearful in praises, doing wonders." (Ex. xv. 11.)

The end which God had in view in the creation of the world, and which he has in view in its government, corresponds with his holy nature and eternal purposes. For aught we know, he may have created as many worlds as there are stars, which in a clear night twinkle in the heavens. These worlds may be inhabited by innumerable moral beings, inferior or superior to us. And the administration of the Divine government in this province of his vast empire may have an influence upon the inhabitants of all other worlds. Should this government, the United States, manifest partiality toward any one of States, it would not be respected by the other States. The end which God has ever had in view is the glory of his holiness. Their honor is the highest object which the great men of this world seek. To obtain it they submit to great privations and hardships. They prefer death to its loss. The following passage gives us a scripture view of the end God had in view in the creation of the world, and which he has in view in the administration of his government.

"And the four beasts (or living creatures) had each of them six wings about him, and they were full of eyes within: and they rest not day and night, saying Holy, holy, holy, Lord God Almighty, who was and is, and is to come. And when those beasts (or living creatures) give glory and honor and thanks to Him that sat on the throne, who liveth forever and ever, the four and twenty elders fall down before him that sat on the throne, and worship Him that liveth forever and ever, and cast their crowns before the throne, saying, "Thou art worthy, O Lord, to receive glory and honor and power; for thou hast created all things, and for thy pleasure they are and were created." (Rev. iv. 8—10.) The happiness of his creatures could not be the end God had in view when none of them existed. Nor could his own happiness be the end; for that could not be increased. Those who are most like God, serve him because they love him. When filled with all the fullness of God, or full of the Holy Ghost, they forgot themselves and their own happiness. Their only desire is to do the will of God. Those who are influenced in the performance of duty only by a fear of future misery or a hope of future happiness, are not holy, and cannot be christians.

5. A knowledge of himself helps the christian to obtain a correct knowledge of God's holiness.

Now, we know that every one whose feelings are strong, whether holy or unholy, is desirous of an opportunity for the expression of them, whether the expression increase his happiness or not. The apostle Paul, in view of the severe trials to which his fidelity exposed him, said, "Woe is me, if I preach not the Gospel." It was not a regard to present or future happiness that moved him, but the Holy Spirit operating in his heart. There was a time when the prophet Jeremiah determined to keep silence, because every one mocked him and treated him with contempt. "I am in derision daily," he said, "every one mocketh me. Then I said I will not make mention of him, nor speak any more in His name; but his word was in my heart as a burning fire shut up in my bones, and I was weary with forbearing and I could not stay." Such is the human mind, that the exercise of its powers is necessary to its continued existence. It is the law of holiness which gives them proper direction, and which subjects them to proper discipline. A pure spirit cannot but be active.

God is a spirit, and the most active in the universe. This must be evident to every one who contemplates his vast works and the extent of his government. Who can have any adequate conception of the exercise of the powers of Him whose government extends to all worlds, to all the vast bodies that roll through the heavens, to the different orders of angels, holy and unholy, to the hundreds of millions of the human race, and to all other of his creatures, animate and inanimate? His knowledge and wisdom and power are every moment required for their preservation. Should he for a moment leave them to depend on themselves, they would cease to be. The man, we know, who possesses great physical power, delights to exercise it. So also the man of uncommon powers of mind loves to display them, and the man of great wealth is pleased to do some great thing, or to give some proof of his munificence. Now, as all the attributes of God are infinite, it is His pleasure to exercise or display them. As holiness in the christian gives a right direction to all his purposes, feelings and actions, and makes them harmonize with the will of God, of whom and through whom, and to whom are all things, so holiness in God makes all his purposes, revelations and works of creation, providence and redemption, correspond with the vast plan which he is executing, and the accomplishment of whose ultimate object, is infinitely distant. It is the holiness of God which gives excellency to his character, and it is the holiness of the redeemed which delights Him. The purposes of God correspond with His holy nature, and the method adopted for the accomplishment of them is holy. The will of God, as made known in the volume of revelation, is the only standard by which we may determine whether we are holy or not, and whether we may hope for heaven or not. The following appears to be a proper view of the holiness of God:

6. The holiness of God does not appear to be a distinct attribute, like knowledge, wisdom, power or goodness. It seems to

have reference to all his attributes, and to result from their harmonious operation, directed to the accomplishment of that noble and glorious object which he ever has in view. It may be considered a universal law, which subjects all things to the Divine will. By this law, the nature of God, his attributes, his revelations, all his works, and the administration of his universal government, all have reference to his ultimate end, his own glory. Though God is self-moved, such is his nature that all his acts are holy. The law of holiness is the law of a great sovereign, and a great empire. By this law all the disorders and evils in the world will be overruled for good.

7. The holiness of God appears more gloriously in the work of redemption than in the work of creation.

Man, the lord of this lower world, was created holy; the law he was required to observe is holy and just and good. Its penalty for disobedience, is everlasting death. When God punished the angels that sinned, he made a glorious display of his justice, which is one manifestation of his holiness. Justice demanded the punishment of man, when guilty of disobedience. Had God treated him as he treated the angels, it would have been another display of his justice. It would have been the punishment of dependent beings, creatures, servants. They might have reasoned, as servants often do, and from a knowledge of facts. If God had a Son, they might say, much more dear to him, yea, infinitely more dear to him than any of his creatures, he would spare him, and not punish him as he does us, if a transgressor of his law, much less, if innocent, and if he should offer to become a substitute for us. The very offer of his Son would be such an expression of his love, that God would accept it as he did the consent of the patriarch

Abraham, to sacrifice his son Isaac. Now when God made known his purposes of grace concerning fallen man, to maintain his authority among the angels, who were not indifferent spectators of transactions doubtless known to them—both to the holy and happy, and the unholy and miserable—it seemed to be necessary that they should see consistency in the administration of the Divine government. As God made a revelation of his mercy, which is a brighter view of his character than was made by the law by which sinning angels were punished, or the law by which apostate man was condemned; it was necessary to be, and appear to be, consistent in the administration of his government, that he should make a more glorious exhibition than before made, of his justice or holiness. Otherwise, how could holy angels see the justice of God in the condemnation of their former companions, or the latter his justice in their punishment? The revelation of the forgiving love of God to fallen man, must have occasioned in the minds of holy angels, perplexity, and have encouraged rebellion, had they not seen justice fully satisfied by the interposition and death of the Son of God. The offer of the Son of God, infinitely more dear to him than any or all his creatures, to endure the penalty of the Divine law in the room of all disposed to trust in him, gave a more glorious view of the justice and holiness of God, than had before been given to holy or unholy angels. The holiness of God strikingly appears in every part of the plan and work of redemption. In the sufferings and death of the second person of the Trinity, we see how much God hates sin and loves holiness. "Where," observes an eminent divine, "did sin ever appear so irreconcilable to God? Where did God ever break out so furiously against iniquity? The Father would have the most excellent person, the next in order to himself, and equal to him in all the glorious perfections of his nature, die on a disgraceful cross, and be exposed to the flames of Divine wrath, rather than sin should live, and his holiness remain forever disparaged by the violations of his law."

The Son of God is the brightness of his Father's glory, and the express image of his person. But man was originally created in the image of God. The image of God in man was only a representation of the character of God, as revealed to him before his apostasy, in the *moral law*. But Christ is the image of God in a higher sense. He corresponds with the *law of faith*, and with all the revelations God has made of himself, both in the law and in the Gospel.

The work of redemption is the great work of God on which his mind is fixed, and on which all holy beings will forever dwell with increasing delight.

When God first made a revelation of his forgiving love, holy angels must have been filled with wonder, as they had seen some of their number on account of their sin, banished from heaven, and reserved in chains under darkness unto the judgment of the great day; it was natural for them to expect that apostate man would in like manner be punished. They could see no way by which God could be just, keep his word and maintain his authority, and pardon transgressors of his holy law. They could not know that God had a Son without a revelation. When, therefore, they understood that God had a Son, and that he was willing to take the sinner's place, and to die in his stead, they were filled with delight and rapture. They clearly saw how the holiness of God could more gloriously appear in the justification of all who believe in Jesus, than in their punishment. The angels that sinned, and who are suffering the wrath of God, cannot bring any charge against him of inconsistency, or accuse him of punishing them without sufficient cause. As much greater, more excellent and more dignified as the second Adam is than the first, so much more gloriously the holiness of God appears in the death of the former, than it could appear in the death of the latter and his posterity. Christianity has not diminished our obligation to obey the moral laws, but has strengthened its authority, and given it lustre. The church of God, redeemed by the blood of Christ, is a holy church. "But ye are a chosen generation," said Peter to the saints whom he addressed, " a royal priesthood, a holy nation, a peculiar people, that ye should show forth the praises of Him who has called you out of darkness into His marvellous light." (1 Pet. ii. 9.) "Know ye not," said the apostle Paul to the church of Corinth, "that ye are the temple of God, and that the Spirit of God dwelleth in you? If any man defile the temple of God, him shall God destroy; for the temple of God is holy, which temple ye are."

REFLECTIONS.

Since it is manifest from the view we have taken of the holiness of God, that his very nature, purposes, affections, acts and works are holy; he must look upon all sin, in any of his creatures, with infinite abhorrence. Man we know was originally created holy, with full power to do the will of God. So long as he continued innocent, God was pleased with him, and loved him. He was the property of God, who created him, and on whom he depended for the continuance of his being. As the holiness of God was manifested in his creation, so his holiness was manifested in his condemnation, and would have been manifested in his punishment, had no provision been made for his redemption. As the moral law was written upon the heart of man, when created, so the law of faith or of grace must be written upon the heart of every one who can please God. It may be a question, perhaps it may be thought a curious question, whether man, had he never sinned, could without some change of nature, have worshiped the three persons in the ever blessed Trinity. It does not appear from the Scriptures, that any revelations of a plurality of persons in the Godhead was made to our first parents before their apostasy. The worship of innocent man must have been very different from the worship of the christian. The humility of the former must have been very different from that of the latter. The former had no consciousness of guilt, could not repent, as he had not sinned—could not believe, as he depended on his own works and not on the works of another for justification, consequently could not present the sacrifice of a broken spirit, a broken and a contrite heart. Now the law of faith or of grace written in the heart of the christian must be different from the law written in the heart of innocent man.—From the treatment the angels who sinned received from their offended Sovereign, we may learn how God views sin, and how he will punish it. They were the creatures of God, were created in His image sustained a nearer relation to Him than children do to their parents, had, for aught we know, faithfully served Him for a long period ; but for transgression of His law, which is holy, just and good, they were banished from heaven, and are now reserved in chains under darkness, unto the judgment of the great day. Now, if we overlook for a moment the expression of God's displeasure, it is manifest that so nicely arranged, adjusted and balanced, is the moral kingdom of God, and in such perfect harmony was the original structure of the moral powers of His subjects, that the natural consequence of sin was remediless ruin. But how could God manifest consistency of character and support His authority, without *an expression* of His hatred of sin, corresponding with His infinite holiness? Admitting that God is infinitely holy, His hatred of sin must be infinite; and how can He express His hatred of sin except by its punishment? The Scriptures assure us as a *matter of fact*, that God has banished the angels that sinned, from heaven, and has reserved them in chains under darkness unto the judgment of the great day, when they will be punished also for their opposition to his Son, and to the church redeemed by his sufferings and death. How dreadful and certain, then, must be the doom of the impenitent sinner, the wrath of an infinite God resting on him forever! how groundless all hope of escape! If the angels that sinned did not escape, how can you, sinner, if you continue impenitent, hope to escape the punishment due to your innumerable transgressions? Pause, and think of these things. Be alarmed in season.

Christianity has not repealed or modified one precept of the moral law. "Think not," said Christ, "that I am come to destroy the law or the prophets; I am not come to destroy, but to fulfil. For verily I say unto you, till heaven and earth pass, one jot or one tittle shall in no wise pass from the law till all is fulfilled." God does not threaten without a fixed determination to execute.

3. The method God has devised and adopted for the justification of the ungodly, gives us the most affecting view of His hatred of sin, and His determination to punish all who refuse to accept the offer of pardon through faith in His Son. "The Father loveth the Son, and hath given all things into his hand.

He that believeth on the Son hath everlasting life, and he that believeth not the Son shall not see life, but the wrath of God abideth on him." "Forasmuch as ye know," said the apostle Peter, " that ye were not redeemed with corruptible things, as silver and gold, from your vain conversation, received by tradition with your fathers; but with the precious blood of Christ, as of a lamb without blemish and without spot." Had not sin appeared to God a great evil, the tendency of which, if unchecked and counteracted, must subvert and ruin His kingdom, He would not have called forth His dearly beloved Son from His bosom, and consented to make him a curse for guilty men to effect their redemption. " He was wounded for our transgressions, he was bruised for our iniquities, the chastisement of our peace was upon Him, and with His stripes we are healed." God could not manifest consistency of character, support his authority, and appear glorious in holiness, in the redemption of any of the human race, without the sufferings and death of one sustaining a nearer relation to Him than any of His creatures. This we can all understand. No parent will punish a beloved son without sufficient cause, much less, if innocent, for the guilty. How can God appear holy to the angels, holy and unholy to the millions and hundreds of millions of the human race, or even to ourselves, should he justify us without full satisfaction for our sins? Justice must be satisfied or we cannot be saved. In ourselves there is no help. God has accepted the offer of His beloved and only begotten Son to be a substitute, and has not spared Him, but has delivered Him for our offences, and raised Him again for our justification. Some, when meditating on the justice and holiness of God, discover nothing amiable in his character, but perceive feelings of opposition awakened. But when their attention is directed to the sufferings and death of His Son, who knew no sin, and who gave His life to save them from death, they discover the strongest proofs of His tender compassion, and earnest desire of their salvation. The language of the Gospel is, to every one of you, "Come, for all things are ready."

The fact of the death of Christ, as well as the fact of the punishment of the angels that sinned, makes it certain that all unbelievers who persevere in unbelief will perish. Can any of you, my hearers, while contemplating the cross of Christ, indulge any hope that you can, without faith in Him, escape the punishment to which your sins expose you? Can you believe that God will not be as good as His word? that He will spare you when He did not spare His only begotten Son, when He stood in the room of sinners? The holiness of God will appear glorious in your condemnation, if not in your salvation.

The time is coming when holiness to the Lord will be upon all his works—upon the gates of that prison where the wicked will suffer His wrath, as well as on the gates of heaven. His holiness will appear glorious in the display of His justice as well as in the display of His mercy. Be persuaded then, my hearers, to be holy as God is holy. If christians, strive to be more holy. If unrenewed, consider this: "Without holiness no man shall see the Lord." Amen.

INCOMPREHENSIBILITY OF GOD.

JOB XI. 7—9.

"Canst thou by searching find out God ? canst thou know the Almighty unto perfection ? It is as high as heaven, what canst thou do ? deeper than hell, what canst thou know ? The measure thereof is longer than the earth and broader than the sea."

When we meditate on the being, the attributes and the works of God, objects vast, deeply interesting and glorious occupy our thoughts, and a scene awfully grand and sublime passes before us, the utmost limits of which the powers of the most vigorous minds cannot reach.

We may be pleased and delighted, when we contemplate the most beautiful productions of art, or the achievements of the renowned of this world, which historians record, and on which poets and orators love to dwell; but how great is the change experienced, when our attention is directed to the marvelous works and mighty acts of God?

We are so constituted that the subjects on which we are accustomed to meditate have a transforming influence. Hence we find that those who are most uniformly devout, are most like God and best prepared to endure without repining, the trials through which they are called to pass. Who can describe the happiness of him, who forgetful of the cares and perplexities, the disappointments and troubles of life, is filled with all the fulness of God?

Few are aware how little they know of God, compared with

what may be known of him. It is a remarkable fact that some who have made the greatest attainments in their knowledge of the laws of the material world, have very imperfect views of him who is a spirit, and who seeketh such to worship him as worship him in spirit and in truth. They are still more ignorant of him who is the brightness of his Father's glory and the express image of his person. The light of nature, however clearly it may shine, gives them no knowledge of Christianity, and no knowledge of a plurality of persons in the Godhead. There is no intimation in the law of nature, or the moral law, of the forgiving love of God. All the knowledge we have of the plan adopted for the redemption of men is derived from revelation. The opinions and conduct of very many prove conclusively that they are ignorant of the character of him who looks upon all sin with infinite abhorrence, and who is determined to punish with everlasting destruction every impenitent transgressor. "The wicked, through the pride of his countenance, will not seek after God: God is not in all his thoughts."

Though our knowledge of God in the present life is extremely limited, yet he has furnished us with the means, by which we may know all that is necessary for us to know in order to our salvation. We may rejoice that in him there are inexhaustible treasures of knowledge, wisdom and goodness, to which all the redeemed have free access. Were not God infinite in all his attributes, we could not understandingly and unreservedly trust in him, or worship him. We shall never, even in the future state, know all that may be known of God. But the revelations he will constantly make of himself and of his purposes, will furnish holy beings with new subjects of meditation, suited to their advancement in knowledge. The treasures of knowledge and wisdom in God may be compared to an immense library, constantly open, and to which additions will continue to be made, as needed by his saints. While in this life we are inexcusable for not endeavoring to know all that may be known of God. Surely, the more we love him, the more desirous we shall be to increase our knowledge of his character and will.

My design in the following discourse is to direct your attention to some particular views of the incomprehensibility of God in connexion with what may and ought to be known of him.

1. *The mode of God's existence* is incomprehensible.

The exercise of our powers, when most active, is confined to a very narrow circle. They cannot fathom the depths of infinity. God is a spirit, and invisible. All our knowledge of him is derived from his word and works. We know that there can be but one infinite being. The word and works of God plainly declare his unity. If we carefully study the Scriptures, we may without difficulty distinguish the true God from all false gods, whether the works of men's hands, or the creatures of their imaginations. The more thoroughly we search the Scriptures, the more we shall be disposed to adopt the language of the text.

Though the diffusion of Christian knowledge has banished from this land all *visible gods made by men's hands*, yet the unrenewed heart is the same in every age, and disposed to worship a god that can be comprehended, rather than him who is incomprehensible. Human reason is made the standard by which many determine what God *ought to be and do*, and what he is and will do.

The Scriptures, which are a revelation from God, as might be expected, contain many things above our reason, the reason of those who have just begun to be; but which cannot be shown to be contrary to the reason of him who is pursuing an object, the accomplishment of which is infinitely distant. Our reason ought to be exercised in ascertaining what God has revealed, believing it to be important truths, whether we understand it or not. Do not little children believe many things said by their parents, which they do not understand?

Many things respecting the mode of God's existence we may understand, and many things are incomprehensible. We can understand that God has existed from eternity; but who can comprehend the eternity of His existence? "A thousand years in His sight are but as yesterday when it is past, and as a watch in the night." We can understand that God is and must be Omnipresent; but who can comprehend Omnipresence? The Omnipresence, Omniscience, Infinite Wisdom, and power of God are necessary for the upholding, support, and government of all things. But who can comprehend any of these attributes? We can understand the declarations that inexhaustible treasures of good are in God—that He is a God of truth—cannot deceive or be deceived—that He is infinitely holy and glorious; but how feeble and limited are our conceptions of these attributes? We can understand that the infinite God is our preserver, sovereign, lawgiver, and judge, and that He is worthy of our supreme love, and ought to be worshiped and obeyed with the full exercise of all our powers. But our conceptions of Him in all these relations are limited, and all attempts to extend our thoughts and meditations beyond the bounds of revelation involve us in total darkness.

Neither the works of creation, nor the laws of nature make known to us the forgiving love of God. It is the law of nature, written in the hearts of all men, according to the principles of which the unrenewed reason. This accounts for the fact that some who, proud of the powers of their own mind, and of their attainments in physical science, neglect the Scriptures, and are unitarians or infidels. The moral law is a transcript of the divine character, as revealed to our first parents before their apostasy; but it contains no intimation of mercy, and of course no intimation of a plurality of persons in the deity. We know that when any are awakened, their first endeavor is to obtain justification and peace by the deeds of the moral law. They never receive understandingly and cordially the doctrine of the trinity till they experience a work of grace in their hearts. The doctrines peculiar to Christianity, which bring to our view a plurality of persons in the deity, must be received on the testimony of God himself. When man was created, and so long as he continued innocent, no revelation was made to him of the forgiving love of God, or of a plurality of persons in the Godhead. Had he continued innocent, he probably would never have had any knowledge of the doctrine of the trinity. A revelation of the Son of God, who saves from sin would have rendered the penalty of the law powerless. God did not say to our first parents, if you disobey my command, you may be forgiven, for I have provided for you a Saviour, who will obey the law for you, and suffer its penalty.

After the apostasy of man, God did make a revelation of Himself, which He had not made to him before, and which could not have been made to him before, without encouraging him to sin. This new revelation did not obscure any that had been previously made, but rather gave lustre and power to His law, which man was required to obey a s the foundation of his justification.

The infinite and incomprehensible God has so revealed Himself in accommodation to the weakness of our understanding, that we are fully authorized to view Him as existing in three persons, having different and distinct offices in the plan and work of redemption, all equal in power and glory, and all one in essence. As God is incomprehensible, it is unreasonable for us to object to the revelations He has made of Himself. God the Father addresses His Son as a distinct and Divine person, having a distinct office to execute. "But unto the Son He saith, Thy throne, O God, is forever and ever; a sceptre of righteousness is the sceptre of thy kingdom. Thou hast loved righteousness and hated iniquity; therefore, God, even thy God, hath anointed thee with the oil of gladness above thy fellows. And thou Lord in the beginning hast laid the foundations of the earth, and the heavens are the work of thy hands. And again, when He bringeth the first begotten into the world, he saith, and let all the angels of God worship Him." (Heb. i. 6–10.) The divinity and distinct personality of the Son of God are clearly revealed in the passage just given. The distinct personality of the Holy Spirit is revealed in the following passage: "And when the Comforter is come," said Christ, "whom I will send unto you from the Father, he shall testify of me." The divinity of the Holy Spirit is declared in the following passage, Acts v. 1–11: "Peter said, Ananius, why hath Satan filled thine heart to lie unto the Holy Ghost? Thou hast not lied unto men, but unto God." It was the Holy Spirit that converted three thousand on the day of Pentecost. Now, how God can exist in three persons, and be but one in essence, is beyond our comprehension. But it is only one of many things in God we cannot comprehend. It is not necessary or safe for us to attempt to go beyond what God has revealed. Secret things belong to Him.

The law we are now required to obey, as the foundation of our justification, is the law of faith. This is a transcript of the character of God as revealed in the gospel. This is a brighter exhibition of the divine perfection than could be made by the moral law. This we cannot understand and obey without a knowledge and belief of the doctrine of the trinity.

Now, we can without any perplexity separately contemplate the perfections, and appropriate the works of the Father, of the Son, and of the Holy Spirit. We can understand that they can execute different offices, which none but divine persons can execute. The doctrine of the trinity, which so perplexes the learned unitarian and infidel, is received with delight by the humble Christian. He can separately contemplate the Father, whose law he has broken; the Son, who by His obedience and death, has become the end of the law for righteousness, and the Holy Spirit, to whom he is indebted for renewing and sanctifying grace. There is a recognition of the doctrine of the trinity in every acceptable prayer offered to God.

Curiosity may urge the proud man to pursue his inquiries farther than the light of revelation extends. But, beyond this limit, on what foundation can he rest, what guide can he follow, of what use can be his reason or his learning? Speculations here are like the discordant theories of philosophers respecting subjects, which the most persevering investigations have not enabled them to understand. Happy is the man, who is satisfied with the revelation God has made, and the language of whose heart is, Lord, what wouldst thou have me to do? The man who refuses to receive any truth except on the evidence of reason, denies the veracity of God. No created mind could ever have thought of such a plan as God has devised and adopted for the redemption of men. Our belief of the doctrines of Christianity must depend on the testimony of God. At a certain time Jesus answered, and said, "I thank thee, O Father, Lord of heaven and earth, because thou hast hid these things from the wise and prudent, and hast revealed them unto babes. Even so Father, for so it seemed good in thy sight."

It may here be added, the right understanding of truths, which have reference to the things of the Spirit and Christian experience, depends rather on the state of the heart, than on the power of the understanding, however highly it may be cultivated.

II. The existence of moral evil under the government of an infinitely holy God, is a subject which must forever be incomprehensible.

When God created the angels, he knew that some would sin, and be ruined. Should the inquiry be made, Why then did He create those he knew would sin and be ruined? who would be able to give any satisfactory answer?

When the angels were created, and created in the image of God, and perfectly holy, he could but love them. They sustained a nearer relation to Him than children do to their parents. They were swift to obey His commands, and delighted to worship Him. Why did not God prevent all, as well as a part of those whom He loved, and who had given proofs of their obedience to his commands, from falling, when He perfectly knew the consequences of sin? Who will dare give an answer? And why did he not provide for them, as well as for man, a Redeemer?

When God created man, he created him in His own image, with full power to do His will. He was perfectly holy, and for a time delighted to worship his Creator. Had not the tempter been permitted to visit the garden of Eden, man, probably, would never have fallen. God certainly loved our first parents as His creatures, who were like Him, only infinitely inferior, so long as they continued innocent. And he knew what would be the consequence, if Satan were permitted to visit the habitation of man. Why, then, some may imagine, did He not prevent the approach of this subtle enemy to Paradise, and thus preserve the millions, and hundreds of millions of the human race from ruin? How could our Creator and Heavenly Father suffer a deceiver and a murderer to enter this peaceful world, while it was the abode of innocence, holiness, and happiness? How could He see those, whom He dearly loved, destroy themselves, and ruin the multitudes of the human race, without an exercise of his power to prevent so great evils? How can we reconcile well known facts with the infinite goodness of God? We can only answer, that God can and does cause light to shine out of darkness, and can and does make the wrath of man to praise Him. We know that the fall of man has given God an *opportunity* to make such a revelation of Himself, as could not have been made, had man continued innocent. Had man never sinned, there would have been no revelation of Him, who saves from sin, and who is the brightness of His Father's glory, and the express image of His person. What knowledge could we have had of the mercy of God, or of His forgiving love, had man never sinned? The love which He has manifested toward His enemies, and the vast provision He has made for the redemption of apostate men, give us brighter views of His perfections than we could have had, if our first parents had continued innocent.

Some things we can understand. It was the will of God that the love of our first parents should be tried. Had they successfully endured the trial, their love would have appeared more excellent and honorable, than if not tried. It is, we know, the trial of any virtue which discloses its excellency and beauty. How can we have a perfect view of the operations of benevolence, without proper occasions of its exercise? How could we have any adequate knowledge of that love which is manifested toward enemies, if no enemies ever existed? It required an exhibition of more intense love to pardon and save sinners than to justify the righteous. The praise of the redeemed will express deeper feelings of love than they could have experienced, had they never been justly exposed to the wrath of God.

III. The method which has been devised and adopted by Infinite Wisdom and benevolence for the redemption of men, is too grand, and too extensive in its bearings and influence, to be comprehended by any finite being. Angels, who have made great attainments in knowledge, desire to look into it. But all those truths, which are essential to our salvation, have been made plain by a variety of familiar illustrations. In this we can but notice the love and condescension of God. Such is the simplicity of the language of the gospel, that young children may, without difficulty, understand it. We may understand what doctrines are revealed and taught, though we may not be able to comprehend them. Who can comprehend the mediation of the Son of God? 1 Tim. iii. 16, " Without controversy," said the great apostle Paul, " great is the mystery of godliness; God was manifest in the flesh, justified in the spirit, seen of angels, preached unto the Gentiles, believed on in the world, received up into glory." " All things," said Christ, " are delivered unto me of my Father; and no man knoweth the Son, but the Father; neither knoweth any man the Father, save the Son, and he to whomsoever the Son will reveal Him." (Matt. xi. 27). Those whose knowledge of the character and works of Christ is most extensive, must admit that He is a person whom they cannot comprehend. It is enough for us to know that He is an all-sufficient Saviour, approved of His Father, and one on whose power, wisdom, and righteousness we may safely depend for justification and salvation. The more perfectly we know Him, the more we shall love and praise Him; and the more sensible shall we be that our knowledge is very circumscribed. When contemplating the occasion and consequences of His sufferings and death, the light of His glory is sometimes overpowering. How intense His love! How boundless His liberality! "Go ye," he said to his disciples, "into all the world, and preach the gospel to every creature?" All of every nation, and without any respect of persons, who believe on Christ, experience that peace which passeth understanding, and that joy which is unspeakable, and full of glory.

Though the capacities of the Christian will forever increase, they will be fully supplied from the infinite fullness there is in God. Who now can make any objection to a plan of redemption which is suited to the condition and wants of all mankind? All who cordially approve it, and receive, without money and without price, the offers of salvation through faith in Christ, are made unspeakably happy in this life, and receive a good title to an inheritance incorruptible, undefiled, and that fadeth not away. Christianity, when cordially embraced, has never proved a failure. It has always fulfilled all its promises. Though we cannot comprehend the system, we may know all that is necessary to be known in order to secure our salvation.

IV. Many facts under the government of God, which relate to the present state and future prospects of our fellow-creatures, are above our comprehension.

As our eye glances over the different parts of the world, we see by far the greater portion of the human race involved in darkness, and ignorant of the volume of revelation, and of the character and works of the Son of God. The light of Christianity, which has been such a blessing to us in this country, shines upon but a small portion of the world. Christians have been faulty, and the church has not done all she could. But shall we overlook the providence of God? Shall we say that any given to Christ in the covenant of redemption have been lost? Thousands and tens of thousands of the most faithful have suffered a martyr's death. Were they not willing to meet dangers, and to do what they could? The most faithful have been most opposed, and most cruelly persecuted. Why did not God protect them, and give greater success to their labors, we know not? Why were the holy apostles so severely tried, and some of them, if not all, put to death for their fidelity? Had the church been more faithful, would she not have been more persecuted, and would not more of her most faithful members have been put to death? Why did 4000 years roll away before the Son of God became incarnate? Why was Abram, who lived among idolaters, called and made the father of a great nation, and distinguished by the favors of God, while all the rest of the world was suffered to remain in ignorance of the truth? The facts recorded we can understand; but we know not how to reconcile them with the infinite goodness of God. What can Christians do, if God withhold his spirit? They cannot convert one soul.

Since an atonement has been made sufficient for all mankind, and since God can be just and the justifier of every one that believeth in Jesus, we cannot see why the Spirit is not poured out more abundantly, and why more are not converted and saved. It is as easy for God to convert a thousand as a hundred—in a single day as in any number of years. Why He leaves so many of His creatures, who sustain a near relation to Him, to perish, we know not.

God could in any past age have increased the number and resources of His church, by the copious effusions of His Spirit —could have disposed them to supply the destitute with the Holy Scriptures, and with faithful pastors. Surely, the protection of His faithful servants from sickness and death, when in the midst of their labors, depends on His providence; and their success in converting men depends on the power of His Spirit.

Even where churches are established, and where the great truths of Christianity are clearly and fearlessly preached, many continue till death without any good hope of future happiness. It is an occasion of grief, and of many tears to the faithful preacher, that he is able to accomplish no more. When the Holy Spirit is poured out on a church and congregation, Christians are always active. And what mighty changes are effected in a few days, when the Holy Spirit descends upon a church. Should the work continue to progress in a town for a few years as it does for a few weeks, every individual would be numbered with the disciples of Christ. Why revivals of religion are not more extensive, more frequent, and more lasting, we know not. Those excitements, produced by human efforts have, there is reason to believe, been productive of more evil than good. During genuine revivals, why, in the same family, one is converted, and another left, we know not. Sometimes the most gay and thoughtless is taken, and the most uniformly serious is left. The greater the number converted, the more Christ is honored.

Why one is called to preach the gospel, while others of equal and even superior powers of mind and undoubted piety are left, we know not. How many facts we notice for which we can give no satisfactory account. What can we do but bow in humble submission to Him, who will give us no account of His matters further than our duty is concerned?

> "He in the thickest darkness dwells—
> Performs His work—the cause conceals;
> But though His methods are unknown,
> Judgment and truth support His throne."

Why God permits the most dangerous errors to prevail, and to be defended by men of talents and power, we know not. We have often seen men distinguished for the powers of their mind and their learning, among the enemies of God. "Woe unto the world," said Christ, "because of offences! for it must needs be that offences come; but woe to that man by whom the offence cometh." But nothing so effectually rouses the friends of the truth to put forth all their powers in its defence, as the propagation of dangerous errors by men of learning. The most eminent Christians have been those who have been most severely tried. The exertions of men in the different departments of life have corresponded with their necessities. Great men have been produced by great occasions, and severe trials of their physical, their mental, or moral powers. In many cases we may, when the darkness is past, see how God can bring good out of evil, and cause the wrath of man to praise Him. The more we know of the character and works of God, the more we admire His wisdom and benevolence, as manifested in the administration of His government, and the more too, we are convinced that we cannot, by searching, find Him out.

REFLECTIONS.

1. In reviewing the subject under consideration, we can but feel that unbounded praise is due to God, who, though infinite in all his perfections, and unsearchable in all His ways, has condescended to make the path of life so plain that way-faring men, though fools, need not err therein. Had God made such a revelation of His gracious purpose, that none but men of learning could understand it, the illiterate must of necessity be excluded from Heaven. If any, therefore, fail of obtaining Heaven, it will not be because they cannot understand the essential truths of Christianity, but because they refuse to perform known duty. No one acts more freely than the sinner, who indulges himself in those practices which darken his understanding, and ruin his soul. Can any one utter the complaint, I would serve God, but I know not how; I would return to Him, but I know not the way? Can any one complain, I would come to Christ, but He will not receive me. Has He not said, "Him that cometh unto me, I will in no wise cast out?"

2. The deepest humility is the result of intense meditation on the character and works of Him, whom no man can by searching find out. What is our knowledge compared with the knowledge of God; what our wisdom, or power, or goodness; what our greatest, or most benevolent acts compared

with his? What small returns we have made to God for all that He has done for us! While some are ever ready to discuss subjects respecting the being, attributes, or government of God, which are above their comprehension, they neglect to perform duties clearly made known and essential to their salvation. The humble Christian finds no insuperable obstacles in the plain path of duty. His only complaint is of his unfaithfulness in his obedience to the known will of God.

3. Our subject should lead us to be much in prayer to God, on whom we depend for success in all our endeavors to do good. In Him we know are inexhaustible treasures. The more frequently and reverently we approach Him, the more ready He is to grant our request. He is as ready to bestow upon us great favors as those of small value. He has said, "Open thy mouth wide, and I will fill it." However deep our sense of our unworthiness, we may ask for great things, if our dependence is on Christ, our surety.

4. It is evident from the view which has been taken of the subject under consideration, that all objections to the ways of God are unreasonable. There was a time when the patriarch Jacob thought all things against him; but afterwards he found that the most painful event was productive of his greatest happiness. As we do not know what end is to be answered by any event of Providence, with what propriety can we find fault with what we cannot understand?

Who can determine how many worlds exist in the boundless regions of space, what relation this world bears to other worlds, and how the administration of God's government in this province may affect other provinces in His vast empire? When we know what ends are accomplished by the mysterious events of time, all the ways of God will appear glorious. When we have existed a thousand, or ten thousand years, we shall begin to understand that vast system, which embraces all worlds, all the measures of duration, and by which God is accomplishing that magnificent and glorious object, whose dazzling brightness we are not now able to behold, but whose splendor will fill the universe with light. The more clearly we see God in every event, the more ardently we shall love Him, and the more zealous, bold, and persevering shall we be in His service.

When the glory of God is unveiled in eternity, the vast assembly of the redeemed will lift up their voice, saying, "Thou art worthy, O Lord, to receive glory, and honor, and power, for thou hast created all things, and for thy pleasure they are, and were created." AMEN.

THE LOVE OF GOD.

JOHN III. 16.

"For God so loved the world, that He gave His only begotten Son, that whosoever believeth in Him should not perish, but have everlasting life."

The text is descriptive of the love which God has manifested toward lost men. The plan he has devised and adopted for their redemption cannot be understood without a knowledge of that law which demands of them perfect obedience as the ground of their justification. This is the law of nature, which is the moral law, and the covenant of works. "It is written in the hearts of all men, their conscience also bearing witness, and their thoughts the meanwhile accusing, or else excusing one another." (Rom. ii. 15.)

This law is founded on the relation man sustains to God as his Creator and rightful Sovereign. "It is holy, and the commandment holy and just and good." And it so exactly corresponds with our nature and constitution, that one sinful action or even thought is sufficient to ruin the transgressor forever. The natural consequence of sin is endless ruin. The transgressor cannot save himself. He is the enemy of Him he has injured. The man who has robbed his neighbor, becomes the enemy of him who was before his friend.

God requires of man nothing more than is perfectly just, nothing more than he was fully able to perform before his apostasy, and nothing which is not connected with his highest happiness. Strict justice is not only the foundation, but the measure of the requisitions of the moral law, and of our obligations to do the will of God.

The moral law was a transcript of the Divine character, as revealed to man before his apostasy. He had then power to discern its excellency, and he then loved and worshiped his Creator with all his heart. Death was the consequence of his disobedience. Any intimation in the Divine law of pardon for transgressors would have rendered its sanction powerless. No one can suppose that God said to Adam, " In the day thou eatest thou shalt surely die ; but if thou eat thereof, thou mayest be forgiven, for I have provided a Saviour for transgressors." Before his apostasy man had no knowledge of Him who saves from sin.

Though the Scriptures teach us that the world was made by the Son of God, yet it does not appear that our first parents, while innocent, had any knowledge of more than one person in the Godhead. The works of creation proclaim the unity of God, but give us no knowledge of the doctrine of the Trinity. The visible heavens declare the glory of the power and wisdom and goodness of God, but not the glory of his forgiving mercy. The doctrines of christianity are not discoverable by the light of nature. They have been made known to us by the light of revelation. The volume of nature is very imperfectly understood without the aid of revelation.

Reasoning from analogy, we must suppose that when God created the angels, He demanded of them perfect obedience to that law which is founded on the relation they sustain to Him as their Creator and rightful Sovereign. When created, they were perfectly holy, loved and served God with all their heart, were swift to obey His commands, and were objects of His delight. So long as they continued obedient they were perfectly happy. One transgression was sufficient to ruin them forever. No Saviour was provided for them. It is written, "and the angels which kept not their first estate, but left their own habitation, He hath reserved in everlasting chains, under darkness, unto the judgment of the great day." Though unutterable misery was the natural consequenc eof sin, yet God, as a righteous Sovereign, could not but express His abhorrence of it. He could not sit an indifferent spectator of any act of rebellion, and continue to be worshiped by holy beings.

Now we cannot see how God could make any other laws for angels and men, than he did make when he created them. They are founded on the relations they sustained to him, they demand of them nothing unreasonable, nothing not connected with their highest happiness. Though they were holy, just and good, they did not exhibit the whole character of God, His forgiving love, the brightest display of His glory. God made to man no revelation of His forgiving love before his apostasy. No offer of pardon was made to the angels that sinned, though they sustained a nearer relation to God than children do to their parents; and while innocent, were objects of His love. They were condemned by that law they transgressed. Apostate man was also condemned by that law he had violated, and was as justly exposed to the wrath of God as were the angels that sinned, and who are now suffering without any hope of ever being pardoned.

Here there is a bound, from which, if we look back, we can discover no way of escape, for men or angels, from deserved punishment. It was perfectly natural for angels, when man sinned, to look for the wrath of God to fall upon him. He himself could expect nothing else but the execution of the penalty of the law he had broken. As yet, God had made no revelation of His forgiving love.

Neither men nor angels could know, without a revelation, that God had a Son; much less that He would be willing to become incarnate, to make Himself of no reputation, and take the place of the transgressor, and suffer death to save him from endless misery. Heaven was filled with wonder when the Son of God, the brightness of His glory, was revealed, and when it was understood that God had purposes of mercy concerning lost men. It was, doubtless, by the influence of one of the fallen angels, that man, of an inferior order, was ruined. This may, perhaps, be one reason why God determined to provide a Saviour for lost men, rather than for the angels that sinned, who knew, from their bitter experience, the awful consequences of rebellion.

When God made a revelation of His forgiving love to men, He did not repeal or modify any portion of the law He had previously given to them. "Do we then make void the law through faith?" said the apostle, "God forbid: yea, we establish the law." (Rom. iii. 31.) The Gospel does not obscure, but adds lustre to the perfections of God, before made known. It is abundantly evident from the Scriptures, that the revelations of God have been progressive. The law we are now required to obey, is the law of faith. This includes the moral law, and is the clearest revelation of it. In the law of faith we see mercy and truth met together, righteousness and peace united. Justice in Christ is satisfied, and the believer is reconciled to God. When God made a revelation to man of His forgiving love, this was a more glorious revelation of His character than had before been made by that law, which is holy and just and good. It is on this account that the Son of

God is declared to be the brightness of His Father's glory, and the express image of His person.

When God punished the angels who transgressed His law, He did not delight in their sufferings. He still loved them as His creatures, but consistency of character, love of holiness, and a regard to His authority demanded the execution of His law. As the law they were required to obey was just, so their punishment was just. A sense of the justice of their punishment makes it intolerable. While they blaspheme the name of God, they know that they ought to love Him.

Can we suppose that there was no mixture of pity in the feelings of God when He punished those whom He once loved, and who, before their apostasy, had long probably been obedient to His commands? May we not suppose that He felt toward them as pious parents feel toward their children, when, from sense of duty they punish them? "Have I any pleasure at all that the wicked should die, saith the Lord God, and not that he should return from his ways and live?" (Ezekiel xviii. 23.)

The punishment of men would have been like that of the angels that sinned, had not God, of His distinguishing goodness, provided us a Saviour. Why He passed by the angels that sinned, and "so loved the world, that He gave His only begotten Son, that whosoever believeth in Him might not perish, but have everlasting life," we know not. It may be, that he chose to provide a Saviour for man, made lower than the angels, that His love might appear more wonderful and glorious. Some particular views may be interesting.

The apostasy of man afforded God an opportunity to make such a revelation of Himself, as could not be made by the works of creation, or by the moral law. He could not offer pardon to those who had never sinned. Nor could He make known to them one who saves from sin and suffering, without giving them some encouragement to sin. The whole character of a good man could never be known, were he never to see any fellow-creature in distress.

TO NOTICE PARTICULARS.

1. It was the pleasure of God to pass by the angels that sinned, and to manifest His forgiving love to fallen and lost men. The transgression of our first parents made them the enemies of God, and rendered it impossible for them, without a change of nature, to discover anything lovely in the Divine character. They sinned without cause. That hatred which is without cause, is the most deadly. Consciousness of guilt did not produce penitence, but only awakened in the minds of our first parents apprehensions of evil, and made them endeavor to hide themselves from their offended Sovereign. By reason of their apostasy they became dead to spiritual life, honor and true happiness. They were, however, the creatures of God, and as such, sustained a near relation to Him. He viewed them with pity, and thought of a method by which He could be just, and save all the truly penitent.

It was when man was expecting every moment that the wrath of an angry God would fall on him, and when holy and unholy angels were looking for his punishment, that the Son of God, the second person in the ever blessed Trinity, and the brightness of His Father's glory, was revealed as the Saviour of lost men. This was a revelation of wonders, and of Him who is wonderful. It was a great event in the administration of the Divine government, and a new era in its history. New views of the character and government of God were presented to the minds of all intelligent beings. New scenes were disclosed intensely interesting to angels and to men.

Though the promise made to our first parents, that the seed of the woman should bruise the serpent's head, was obscure, yet it probably was at the time so explained, that they had a proper knowledge of the object of their faith. By faith, Abel offered a more acceptable sacrifice than Cain. The light which shone on our first parents, compared with that now enjoyed, was like the dim twilight of the morning compared with the clear light of day. The institution of sacrifices, which pointed to that great sacrifice, which Christ offered when he offered up Himself, was suited to make a powerful impression on the minds of our first parents and their posterity. It taught them that they deserved death, and must look out of themselves to God for salvation. Those who became pious in the earliest ages of the world, were as much indebted to the agency of the Holy Spirit, as any are at the present day for renewing grace.

The plan God devised and adopted for the redemption of men, is equally honorable to Himself and safe for us. It could not have originated in any creature, however exalted. It is above the thoughts and beyond the comprehension of any created being. It cannot be understood without some knowledge of the Trinity—a doctrine not discoverable by the light of nature. It is a most glorious manifestation of the love which God exercises toward this fallen race. God, the Father, is the person, whose law man has broken; God, the Son, is the person who has given Himself to redeem us; God, the Holy Spirit, is the person whose office it is to renew the hearts of all given to Christ in the covenant of redemption. All the persons in the Trinity are equally concerned in the salvation of lost men. Holy angels are ministering spirits to Christ and to the church.

2. No language is sufficient to describe the love which God has manifested toward this rebellious world. This the inspired writer understood, when he said, " God *so loved the world*,"—and without attempting any other description than the following—" that He gave His only begotten Son, that whosoever believeth in Him should not perish, but have everlasting life." The measure of the love of God, is the gift of His Son. This is the unspeakable gift of God. This gift is infinitely more valuable than any creature or all creatures, and His works greater than any creature or all creatures could ever perform.

The language of the text is so plain, that way-faring men, though fools, need not err therein. It is understood by all devoted christians who are not influenced by human theories. The relation parents sustain to their children, and children to their parents, are as well understood by the illiterate as by the learned. They know how dear an only son of great promise is to his parents. Much stronger is the love which the latter exercise toward the former, than they can exercise toward servants, however obedient. Much greater is the difference, if the latter are disobedient.

When servants are punished with no greater severity than they deserve, they seldom feel and acknowledge that their punishment is just. They persuade themselves that their master is unfeeling, unnecessarily cruel and tyrannical; that he would not punish a beloved son, if equally guilty, with the same severity. The angels that sinned, no doubt thought that there was no mixture of pity in their punishment, and that there was no necessity for any such punishment as God inflicted on them. But when it was revealed to them that God had a Son, only begotten and dearly beloved, the brightness of His glory, and the express image of His person, who was willing to become a substitute for lost men, and that His Father would not forgive any of the human race without the obedience and death of His dearly beloved Son, they were convinced that sin did appear to God to be a great evil, and that He did not punish any because He delighted in their suffering, but to manifest to the universe His hatred of sin, and his love of holiness.

The Scriptures teach us that the Son of God sustains the same relation to His Father, as the son of an earthly parent sustains to him. This is the view of the subject presented to the mind of every christian, when he listens to the sound of the Gospel, or searches the Scriptures. It was His Son, dearly beloved and only begotten, whom God gave to be the Saviour of lost men. It was the Son of God who magnified the Divine law, and made it honorable by His obedience and death. It is the Son of God who is seated at the right hand of His Father, making intercession for all who trust in Him. The Son of God is the Lord, whom we are bound to obey, and who will be the Judge of the world. No defect can now be discovered in the administration of the Divine government, even in the punishment of transgressors of His law. It is the righteousness of the Son of God which is of infinite value, which is imputed to believers as the foundation of their justification. They can trust themselves in His hands for time and for eternity.

Unless we admit the Divinity of the Son of God, who became the substitute for sinners by His obedience and death, we cannot understand the text, or feel satisfied with the foundation of our hope. Unless we admit that it was the eternal Son of God, who magnified the Divine law and made it honorable by His obedience and death, our views must be very limited of the mercy and grace of God, displayed in the redemption of men. "He that spared not His own Son, but delivered Him up for us all, how shall He not with Him also freely give us all things?" (Rom. viii. 32.)

3. One of the objects which the Son of God had in view in assuming human nature, was to make it manifest to the universe that He was the Saviour of lost men, and not of the angels that sinned. "For verily He took not on Him the nature of angels, but He took on Him the seed of Abraham. Wherefore in all things it behooved Him to be made like unto His brethren, that He might be a merciful and faithful High Priest, in things pertaining to God, to make reconciliation for the sins of the people." (Heb. ii. 16, 17.) Had He not been God manifest in flesh, how could we have discovered any proof of His love of lost men, and also of the depth of His pity? His human nature is the medium through which we know the feelings of His heart. By His Divine nature He is one with God, and by His human nature He is one of us. "He is the way, the truth and the life." We can approach God and find access to Him, only through faith in Christ; and all the blessings we enjoy come to us through this medium. Had He appeared in a shining and glorious form, who could have freely conversed with Him, or have ventured to be one of His associates? It was the Son of God that magnified the Divine law, by His obedience and death—that made an atonement of infinite value to effect the redemption of lost men. It was the Son of God that said, "My soul is exceeding sorrowful, even unto death"—that fell on His face in the garden of Gethse-

mane, and prayed, saying, "O my Father, if it be possible, let this cup pass from me, nevertheless, not as I will, but as thou wilt." In His agony, "his sweat was as it were great drops of blood falling down to the ground." It was the Son of God, whose Father hid His face from Him, when He was on the cross, that He might perform the work of the second person in the Trinity alone, and receive the honor to which it entitled Him.

4. Thus it appears that in the promotion of the glory of His holiness, God does not lay all the burden on His creatures, while He sits upon His throne, unmoved. He performs infinitely the most important part of this work. God does not receive honor for that which has cost him nothing. He is not like the commander of a great army, who does nothing more than direct his forces, and who has no pity for the wounded and suffering. And He is not like a king, who sits in his palace unmoved, when many of his subjects are in distress. He is like the king who pities his suffering subjects, and can sympathize with them; who cannot behold their tears without being affected. Or He is like the commander of an army, who is seen in the field of battle, and who exposes himself to the greatest danger. Such a person is deserving of praise. Such an one we admire; but despise him who does not submit to any hardships, and does not sympathize with the suffering. For what was the Son of God revealed, if not by his mediation, to exhibit brighter views of the Divine character than ever had before been exhibited? Why should not our Creator, and Lord, perform an important part in that great work, the object of which is His own glory, the glory of His holiness? Much of the opposition to the Divine character arises from such representations of it, as make the impression

on the minds of many, that God does not pity lost men, especially when He punishes them. But a proper view of the sufferings of the only begotten Son of God is suited to correct the impression. Can God love His creatures, and be unmoved when He beholds their tears, and hears their cries? And do not the depth of His sympathy, and the greatness of the sufferings of His Son correspond with the strength of His affection? It is written, in all their afflictions He was afflicted, and the angel of His presence saved them; in His love, and in His pity He redeemed them. And He bare them and carried them all the days of old.

5. Man, the Scriptures teach us, was made in the image of God, and in his most perfect state was like Him, only infinitely inferior. What can we know of God except from the revelations He has made of Himself in His word and works? Man is that work of God, by which we learn that God is a person, and by which we may obtain just conceptions of His moral perfections. Now it must be acknowledged that those who have made the greatest attainments in holiness are most like God—and most susceptible of being affected by a view of the sufferings of their fellow-creatures, though they do not sustain so near a relation to them as they do to God, their Creator. It must be confessed that the most pious have always been most ready to sympathize with the suffering, and to make efforts for their relief. God, who is infinitely holy, is the most compassionate Being in the universe, and the most susceptible of being moved by a view of the sufferings of His creatures. He hears their cries, and beholds with tender compassion their tears. Though angry with the wicked, He is long suffering toward them, not willing that any should perish, but that all should come to repentance. It is God, who clothes

the naked, feeds the hungry, heals the sick, and saves all who believe in Christ, whom He has given for our redemption.

6. It seems to be the opinion of some that a state of quietude is essential to the happiness of God. Can any suppose that a state of perfect quietude is essential to the happiness of God—that He is unmoved by those events which produce the greatest distress among men? This is not the Scripture view of the character of God, or of good men most like Him.

May we not suppose that the accomplishment of great and glorious objects by appropriate means is essential to the happiness, as well as to the glory of God? What contributes so much to the happiness and honor of men, as success in the pursuit of objects of great value? And their happiness and honor are often in proportion to the difficulties they have overcome, and the hardships they have endured. Great men and great nations rejoice, when, by great labors and great sacrifices, they have obtained objects of great value. Why did the British nation rejoice when they gained the victory of 1815, which cost immense sums and the lives of many distinguished officers, and thousands of brave men? Why did this nation rejoice when they obtained their independence, which cost them much blood and treasure? Now who can estimate the value of the object God is pursuing by the mediation of His Son, and the agency of His Spirit? The means employed correspond with the greatness and excellency of the object. Is it any more strange that God should give His Son to suffer and die, than that He should punish with everlasting destruction multitudes of His creatures, who sustain a near relation to Him? I see nothing in the revelations God has made of Himself inconsistent with the belief that the exercise of the noblest feelings is essential to his highest happiness. The work which the Son of God left heaven to accomplish must appear to all intelligent beings, who understand it, to be great, honorable, and glorious. The grandeur of the object of pursuit, the wisdom and benevolence of the plan, and the exalted thoughts of the chief agent, are far above the comprehension of any creature. The Redeemer had a perfect understanding of the work before He commenced it. He had power to lay down His life, and to take it again. He was perfectly voluntary in undertaking the work He successfully accomplished.

The reward which the Son of God has received in Heaven is for what He has done. "And I beheld," said John, " and I heard the voice of many angels round about the throne, and the beasts (or living creatures), and the elders, and the number of them was ten thousand times ten thousands and thousands of thousands, saying, with a loud voice, Worthy is the Lamb that was slain, to receive power, and riches, and wisdom, and strength and honor, and glory, and blessing. And every creature which is in heaven and on the earth, and such as are in the sea, and all that are in them, heard I saying, Blessing, and honor, and glory, and power be unto Him that sitteth upon the throne, and unto the Lamb forever and ever." (Rev. v. 11–13.) God will allow no creature to rob Him of His glory.

REFLECTIONS.

It is evident from the view which has been taken of the subject under consideration, that those most like God, and most distinguished for piety, are most susceptible of being affected by a view of the unhappy condition of their fellow-creatures— most willing to submit to great hardships, and to make great sacrifices for their salvation. They are most like Him who, though rich, became poor for our sakes, and who gave His life to purchase our redemption. Men of deep piety are certainly men of deep feelings, and men of deep feelings cannot but manifest them in various ways. Those who, with cold insensibility, contend for the truths, though their arguments may be strong, have not the spirit of Christ. As their hearts appear to be unaffected, they make the impression on the impenitent that they do not fully believe the doctrines for which they earnestly contend, or that they do not think them very important. But if we know from our own experience the truths for which we contend, and express them with a deep and feeling sense of their importance, we do persuade men. It is a complaint of many that God is represented as an unfeeling Sovereign, who hates the sinner, and punishes him with no mixture of pity. It is true God hates sin, but pities the sinner, whom He is obliged to punish.

2. From the view which has been taken of the subject under consideration, we may conclude that there is nothing too great for God to do for them that love Him. That righteousness which is imputed to the believer is the foundation not only of his hope of justification, but of his hope of future life and glory. In our present state we have only an earnest and a foretaste of the happiness, which all believers will enjoy beyond the grave. The promises of God are sure. In this life we have but a very imperfect knowledge of their import. There is no fiction in the word of God. The truths of Christianity are solemn realities. God has given the most abundant proofs that His love of the world is real, sincere, deep, and holy. "Eye hath not seen, nor ear heard, neither have entered into the heart of man the things which God hath prepared for them that love Him."

3. Infinitely great are our obligations to God, who hath done great things for our redemption. God has but one Son, dearly beloved, and only begotten; the brightness of His glory and the express image of His person. Him he has given, not only to be a teacher and a prophet, but to be offered a sacrifice for us. Had the Son of God been unwilling to suffer in our stead, not one could have been saved. His Father, though he loved Him with infinite affection, did not spare Him when He stood in the room of sinners. When he was upon the cross, crowned with thorns, and treated with every indignity; when He most needed some expression of His Father's love, his Father hid his face from him. He could not use the same language He had been accustomed to use—My Father, my Father—but only, My God, my God; language proper for a malefactor; "My God, my God," He said, "why hast thou forsaken me?" Can we do too much or suffer too much to express our love of Him, who has done and suffered so much for us? When we compare what we have done for Him, with what He has done for us, we must feel that our services have been very deficient, and that we have abundant cause for deep humiliation. Wonderful is the love God has manifested for transgressors of His law. Wonderful is the love of his Son, who has magnified it, and made it honorable by His obedience and death. It is incomprehensible—infinite. We shall never in our meditations be able to reach its height, or depth, or length, or breadth. But meditation, intense meditation on the love of God, manifested in the work of redemption, is suited to move and soften the feelings of our heart, and to strengthen the cords which bind us to Christ.

4. From the view we have taken of the subject under consideration, it is evident that God will execute His law. Though

God is infinitely merciful, He is no more merciful than He was when He punished the angels that sinned, for whom He provided no Saviour. If God did not spare His dearly beloved and only begotten Son, when he stood in the room of sinners, how can any expect that He will spare them, if they persevere in impenitence and unbelief. Do not imagine that God is an unfeeling Sovereign, because He has determined that He will maintain His authority by the execution of His law. Should He neglect to do this, holy beings would cease to adore and worship Him; and Heaven itself would be a place of misery. Though God hates sin wherever He discovers it, yet He loves His creatures, who sustain a nearer relation to Him than children to their parents.

Though our Divine Lord has ascended into Heaven, yet He is present with us by His Spirit. He is in this house, and is near to every one of you. He notices your feelings toward Him; He hears all your objections to the truth, and all your excuses for the delay of repentance. Could you see Him, you would see Him weeping over the sinner still under sentence of condemnation. Could you hear Him speak, you would hear Him say, "Come, for all things are ready," and "Come unto me, all ye that labor and are heavy laden, and I will give you rest." "Him that cometh unto me I will in no wise cast out." "There is no other name given under Heaven among men, by which you can be saved."

Before I close this discourse, let me propose the question to you. Now, after you have heard so much of the love of God, and the great things He has done for you, sinner, will you become a disciple of His dearly beloved Son? This is the question which is presented to your mind every Sabbath. Think of it, and of its immense importance, and if you can do no more, say, from your heart, Lord, I believe, help thou mine unbelief. AMEN.

BRIGHTNESS OF HIS FATHER'S GLORY.

HEBREWS I. 3.

"Who being the brightness of His glory, and the express image of His person."

I SEE not how any one, who rejects the doctrine of the trinity, the divinity of Christ, the necessity of an atonement of infinite value, or the doctrine of justification by faith, can understand the text. It is very imperfectly understood by many of the professed friends of God. To those, who have not been renewed and taught by the Spirit of God, however distinguished they may be for the powers of their mind and their extensive learning, it is one of the most mysterious passages in the whole volume of revelation.

How, it may be asked, can the Son of God be the brightness of His Father's glory? Does not this make Him in some sense superior to His Father? Can we discover excellencies in the character of the Son, more to be loved and admired than any we discover in the character of His Father?

How can Christ crucified, who was unto the Jews, His own people, a stumbling-block, and unto the Greeks foolishness, be the brightness of the glory of the infinitely holy God? How can that object, which to the proud men of the world appears to be the darkest and least attractive, be in reality the most beautiful and glorious? Such inquiries are doubtless suggested to the minds of many who desire to look into these things; and, because satisfactory answers have not been given, they have embraced dangerous and pernicious opinions, and rejected the most essential doctrines of Christianity. To answer these inquiries is the design of the following discourse.

1. Let us first take a view of the revelations God made to man when he was created, and before his apostasy.

The works of creation and Providence proclaimed, and still proclaim the unity of God, His power, wisdom, and goodness. "The heavens," said the psalmist, "declare the glory of God, and the firmament showeth his handy work. Day unto day uttereth speech, and night unto night showeth knowledge." Ps. xix. 1, 2. Great and marvelous are the works of God, sought out of all them that have pleasure therein.

Man was created in the image of God, in righteousness and true holiness. He was like God, only infinitely inferior. He was made but little lower than the angels, and was capable of worshiping God with an understanding heart. He had power to discover and to admire the moral excellency of the divine character. He could discover unity of design not only in the creation, but in the government of the world; in the works of creation and providence he could discover innumerable proofs of the power, wisdom, and goodness of his Creator.

The relation he sustained to God as his creator, benefactor, and rightful sovereign, was the foundation of his obligation to love and serve Him with all his heart. God, as a righteous sovereign, could require nothing less of him than perfect obedience to all his commands. The moral law, which is holy, and just, and good, was written upon his heart, and is now written upon the hearts of mankind. The understanding and conscience of man, when innocent, were sufficient to teach him his duty of perfect obedience.

Nothing was required of him which he was not able to perform, and which was not connected with his highest happiness. The moral law, strict as it is, only pointed out the way by which he might avoid what would injure him, and secure for himself the greatest good. It was, in fact, the shortest and safest path to life and glory.

Now, we never see in any law an intimation of the pardon of transgressors. The sanction of a law is its penalty. The obedient may claim protection, and every good government is bound to give it. God said to Adam, "Of every tree of the garden thou mayest freely eat, but of the tree of knowledge of good and evil thou shalt not eat of it, for in the day thou eatest thereof thou shalt surely die." (Gen. ii. 16, 17.) At a much later period God said—"Cursed is every one that continueth not in all things written in the book of the law to do them." (Deut. xxvii. 26.)

Had Adam continued innocent, he could not have discovered any thing in the works of creation and providence, or in the moral law, to suggest in his mind the idea of a plurality of persons in the Godhead. He discovered abundant proofs of the unity of God, and of his personality. He could but feel his dependence on God and his accountability.

How could he know without a revelation that God had a Son? God would not make a revelation of His Son, who saves from sin, before man had sinned. Our first parents, while innocent, had knowledge of but one person in the Godhead. No one can suppose that God gave any intimation to Adam, while innocent, that if disobedient, he might hope for pardon.

Now the moral law, which contains no intimation of the forgiveness of transgressors, is a transcript of the divine character, *as revealed to man before his apostasy.* Perfect obedience was demanded as the only ground of justification. Justice was the measure of God's claims on man, and man's obligation to Him.

2. In the exercise of forgiving love, a regard to His own glory as a righteous sovereign, made it necessary for God to exhibit His justice as clearly as in the punishment of the angels that sinned. Without a regard to consistency of character, how could God support His authority, and claim the obedience, praise, and adoration of intelligent moral subjects? God must manifest His hatred of sin as well when he pardons the guilty, as when he punishes any of them. To punish the angels that sinned, and to pardon guilty men without an adequate atonement, would destroy all respect for the character and government of God.

Here we may pause, and notice the bound in the revelations God made of Himself before the fall of man. As yet God had given no intimation of His forgiving love. His whole character was not revealed. His brightest perfections were unknown. His mercy was not revealed till there was an occasion for its exercise. His holiness, justice, truth, and goodness were known to our first parents in the garden of Eden. Now we may respect a man who is strictly just, but we love and respect one who is not only just, but compassionate and forgiving. A faithful sovereign must not only be just, but must require his subjects to be just. God, as a holy and righteous sovereign, was obliged to exact perfect obedience of all His subjects. He could not otherwise maintain His authority.

3. The apostasy afforded God an opportunity for such a revelation of His character as had never before been made. The fall of man extinguished that light, by which he had before been able to discover the glory of God in His law and in

His works. The light within him became darkness. As he had no knowledge of but one person in the Godhead, and that person terrible in justice, what could he expect but deserved punishment. His conscience condemned him, and filled his mind with the most distressing apprehensions of evil. Who can form any conception of the gloom and darkness of that day when man partook of the forbidden fruit?

When God created man in His own image, and made him lord of this lower world, holy angels were, no doubt, delighted to unite with this new order of intelligent beings in the worship of God. "The morning stars sang together, and all the sons of God shouted for joy." A new world was made known to them, from visits to which they anticipated much satisfaction. How greatly must they have been shocked when the sad tidings of man's apostasy reached them! They looked for his immediate punishment, and perhaps for the destruction of the world in which he had been placed. Apostate man! though condemned by his own conscience, had no desire to return to God by repentance. He even hated him, whom without cause he had injured. That hatred that is without cause is the most deadly. He could no longer discover any thing lovely in the character of God, whom by his disobedience he had made his enemy.

4. Now let us contemplate the revelations God made of himself and of his gracious purposes after the fall of man, which had not been made to our first parents when innocent. When holy and unholy angels were looking for the wrath of God to fall upon apostate man, and when he, self-condemned, was endeavoring to hide himself from his injured and offended Creator, a light, brighter than any before seen in heaven or on earth, burst from the throne of the Most High. This was the

light of the glory of His forgiving love. This was a new revelation of the purposes of God. It was never before known that God could appear to be righteous, and forgive any transgressor. It was never before known that God had a Son co-essential and co-eternal with Himself, and that He could reveal Himself as existing in three persons—equal in power and glory. The revelation God has made of His love, is not a revelation of any change in Himself, but only a revelation of perfections never before known. The compassion of a man is not known till he has some occasion for its exercise. God has from eternity been as merciful as He is now. There has never been any real change in His character. He is constantly revealing Himself to His church by His providence and by His Spirit. No two periods of the church are exactly alike. Though the character of true Christians may be alike in every thing essential, yet they may exhibit some shades of difference.

Why God passed by the angels that sinned, and provided a Saviour for lost man we know not. The angels that fell sinned against greater light than man enjoyed when innocent, and were a superior order of beings. The redemption of fallen man, made lower than the angels, more gloriously displays, than the redemption of fallen angels, the wonderful condescension and grace of God.

When God made a revelation of His forgiving love, a new chapter in the volume of His revelations, containing wonderful things, was given to be read by all intelligent beings. Holy angels desired earnestly to look into these things. In this chapter we find recorded by God Himself—that He has a Son, who is mediator between guilty man and their offended Sovereign—that He has taken the place of sinners—has been approved by His Father, and has wrought out a righteousness, sufficient to satisfy the demands of the broken law for all who trust in Him.

How the Son of God can be a distinct person and not a distinct being, no one can explain the mystery. "All things," said our Lord, "are delivered unto Me of my Father, neither knoweth any man the Father, save the Son, and he to whomsoever the Son will reveal Him." (Matt. xi. 27.) We ought to be satisfied with the declarations and testimony of God who cannot be deceived, and who will not deceive us. If we adopt the language of Scripture, we are safe.

The humble christian, whose education is limited, experiences no perplexity in addressing the Father, whose law he has transgressed, the Son, who has made an atonement for him, and the Holy Spirit, who has given him a new heart. In every prayer the christian addresses the three persons in the Godhead, and yet understands that he is worshiping but one God.

Without contemplating God as existing in three persons, we can have no consistent view of the plan of salvation. Without believing each person to be Divine, how can we place unlimited confidence in them? The union of the three equal persons in the Godhead, is a firm foundation, on which rests the believer's hope of future happiness and glory.

5. In Christ crucified we have the clearest views of the justice, the truth and the mercy of God. They may be compared to the sun's rays, which, when collected and brought to a focus by a convex mirror, produce intense heat and dazzling brightness. *In this sense, Christ crucified is the brightness of His Father's glory, and the express image of His person.* It is this view of Christ crucified, which is so painful to the unrenewed, and which has been most successful in the conversion of sin-

ners. It is this view, likewise, which moves the best feelings of the believer, and which kindles his love to a flame. "In Christ, mercy and truth are met together, righteousness and peace have kissed each other." (Ps. lxxxv. 10.)

The holiness of God does not appear to be a distinct attribute. It extends to the whole character of God, His purposes, His law, and the administration of His government. It makes all things subservient to His glory. And the glory of His holiness is His ultimate end, the accomplishment of which must be infinitely distant.

The manifestation of strict justice is essential to the support of the government of God, who must be viewed as a Sovereign, acting in view of all His subjects. It seems not to be understood by many, that God, as a faithful Sovereign, must demand perfect obedience of all His subjects, and must, to satisfy justice, and to be respected by the obedient, punish every transgressor. Do not we most respect that government which affords the most perfect protection to the obedient, and which with impartiality punishes every transgressor? Is it not admitted that fewer crimes are known under such a government, than under a lax administration? Let it not be forgotten, that in order to be loved, adored and worshiped, God must manifest, in view of all His subjects, consistency of character. We see in the death of the Son of God, how much His Father regarded strict justice in the administration of His government. When the Son of God stood in the room of sinners, as their substitute, His Father did not spare Him. He withdrew His protecting hand from Him, suffered Him to be betrayed, condemned and led away to the place of execution. When in agony in the garden of Gethsemane, He prayed, if possible, that the cup might pass from Him; His Father did not grant His request. His disciples forsook Him when the powers of darkness were suffered to prevail against Him. When nailed to the cross, crowned with thorns, and reviled by His enemies, His Father hid His face from Him. Great was the triumph of the justice and truth of God, when His beloved Son, in the room of His people, suffered the accursed death of the cross. The claims of the Divine law are now freely satisfied, and the truth of God appears in the justification of all who believe in Christ. It was necessary that the Divine law should be executed on the transgressor, or on an approved substitute. The death of Christ was a great event, more glorious in its consequences than the creation of the world—the earth shook, the rocks were rent, the graves were opened, all heaven was filled with praise of God, and of His beloved Son. The wicked triumphed, but their triumph was short. They soon found that they were defeated.

The mercy of God toward transgressors of His law, gloriously appears in the death of His Son. What stronger proof could He give of His love of the human race, and His readiness to pardon and save them in the only way in which he can consistently do it. We ought not to desire Him to sacrifice His authority, and to involve His whole kingdom in perplexity and confusion, by saving any in their sins. And no one can feel satisfied with the foundation of his hope, unless he can see how in his justification the demands of the Divine law are fully satisfied, and how the truth of God can clearly appear. The intelligent christian admires the plan God has devised and adopted for His redemption. The more he meditates upon it, the more clearly he sees that it is the result of infinite wisdom and benevolence.

Now, when we consider the dignity of the Son of God—His

near relation to His Father, the excellency of His character, His readiness to offer Himself a sacrifice, to honor that holy law man had broken, that He might save the penitent, how terrible must be the justice of His Father, who did not spare Him when He stood in the room of sinners, and how dreadful must be the punishment of those, who have not only broken the law in innumerable instances, but have made light of the offers of mercy through faith in Christ? Though the mercy of God, gloriously appears in the plan adopted for our redemption, yet we find it united with justice and truth. They are not obscured, but are made to appear more glorious, and more worthy of our love by the manifestation of the mercy of God.

Because God is merciful, many, solely on this ground, hope to be saved. They overlook the justice and truth of God, which clearly appeared in the crucifixion of His beloved Son. They do not consider that they must have fellowship with Christ in His sufferings—must feel the condemning sentence of the law in themselves, must see the justice and truth of God in their condemnation, must be convinced that they must perish, unless they cordially accept the substitute God has provided for them. Those who cannot see how God can be just in their condemnation and punishment, and who cannot bear to hear the whole truth, have no good hope of salvation. The most painful truths are most successful.

When it is said that the Son of God is the brightness of His Father's glory, and the express image of His person, the word person, in this connexion, is not to be understood as applicable only to the first person, in distinction from the other persons in the ever blessed Trinity, but as including the whole Godhead as revealed in the plan of redemption.

APPLICATION.

1. It is manifest from the fact of the death of Christ, when He stood in the room of sinners, that God is determined to execute His law. Were it not necessary, He would not have permitted Him to be crucified. God could not appear righteous to all the subjects of His vast kingdom, should He pardon and justify any of the human race without the obedience and death of an approved substitute. The righteousness of Christ, being God as well as man, is of infinite value, and sufficient for the whole human race, if disposed to trust in Him. He felt, when in agony in the garden of Gethsemane, that it was impossible for His Father to save any of the human race without His death. "My soul is exceeding sorrowful, unto death;" He said to those with Him, "tarry ye here and watch. And He went forward a little, and fell on the ground and prayed, if it were possible the hour might pass from Him." (Mark xiii. 34, 35.) Had it been possible, His Father would have accepted His offer as He did that of Abraham, when he was prepared to sacrifice His beloved son Isaac. God will most assuredly execute His law upon all who do not take refuge in Christ. Great must be their guilt who have the Gospel, and reject the offer of mercy.

It will be more tolerable in the day of Judgment for the heathen, who never heard of Christ, or of any way of salvation, than for those who have the Scriptures in their own language, and preachers sent to them to persuade them to trust in Him who saves from sin, and yet who persevere in unbelief. What would be your feelings should you hear of a family in great distress, and should you make very liberal provisions for their relief, and, in addition to this, should you perform a very perilous journey to reach their abode—what, I say, would be your feelings, should they, after being acquainted with your benevolent errand, reject your offer and treat you with contempt? Would you not say, " Let them suffer—they deserve to suffer?"

2. Those who have no knowledge of God, except what they derive from His works of creation and providence, may be learned astronomers, geologists, chemists and philosophers, but have no conception of the brightest perfections of the Divine character. They may be pleased with well written discourses on the attributes of God as discoverable from the light of nature, and may also be pleased with discourses on the precepts of the moral law. But they never wish to hear preached the doctrine of the cross. They do not search the Scriptures, and do not feel their need of the volume of revelation. With the holy Scripture at their command, they choose to follow only the dim light of nature, which gives them no knowledge of the way of salvation through faith in a crucified Redeemer. They shut their eyes to the light which directs the believer on his way to glory.

3. From the view which has been taken of the subject under consideration, we see why the preaching of Paul, and of all others who were determined to know nothing but Christ and Him crucified, was, and ever has been so successful, and so much opposed by many, and many of the learned and wealthy. The doctrines of the cross not only give us the clearest and brightest views of the Divine character, but give the most painful and mortifying views of the depravity of the human heart. No one can understandingly receive the doctrines of the cross, without confessing that he is justly condemned by the Divine law, and justly exposed to everlasting death. It is not difficult to come to this conclusion. If it was

necessary for the Son of God to die in our room that we might have the offer of pardon, then we deserve death. But who, unless the subject of the operations of the Holy Spirit, will confess that he deserves death. This he must understand and confess if he would receive Christ as his Saviour. "We preach Christ crucified," said Paul to the Corinthians, "unto the Jews a stumbling block, and unto the Greeks foolishness; but unto them which are called, both Jews and Greeks, Christ the power of God and the wisdom of God." (1 Cor. i. 23, 24.) This great apostle knew what means were best suited to affect his hearers, and what God was most disposed to bless. No one of the apostles accomplished so much for his Redeemer, and no one was more persecuted.

Looking at Christ crucified, we see how God regards His law, how He views transgressions of it, how much He loves the world and how much He has done for our redemption. If we admit that the atonement is of infinite value, then God must view sin with infinite abhorrence, and how can He express His infinite abhorrence of sin except by executing His law on the transgressor or his substitute? When any indulge hard thoughts of God, who threatens with everlasting destruction the transgressor of His law, let them look at Christ crucified, and all their objections will be swept away.

To conclude. Ample provision, sinner, has been made for your redemption. The offer, without money and without price, is now made of eternal life. Will you not receive it as a gift? Are you unwilling to receive it because it is a gift, and because you must be wholly indebted to the grace of God for the hope of salvation? Oh, be persuaded to confess your sins and your poverty, and to accept the offer freely made while you may. The present opportunity will soon be gone forever.

And you who have a hope that you are christians, think often of the great things which have been done for you, and the bright prospects before you. May a sense of your obligations to your Saviour make you feel that you cannot do too much to advance His kingdom. Amen.

TRAVAIL OF THE SOUL

ISAIAH LIII. 11.

"He shall see of the travail of his soul, and be satisfied."

When that great work *is finished* in which all holy beings are interested, the Son of God, who is performing the most difficult and important part, will look back upon the world, recollecting all his labors and sufferings, and, having perfectly accomplished all his purposes, will be satisfied. The objects obtained will correspond with the plan adopted and the means employed. God will be glorified, and many will be saved, who will be made partakers of the joy and glory of their Redeemer. "The Spirit itself," said the Apostle, "beareth witness with our spirit, that we are the children of God; and if children then heirs, heirs of God and joint-heirs with Christ; if so be that we suffer with Him that we may be glorified together." (Rom. viii. 16–18.) In heaven Christ will appear to be infinitely glorious. To behold His glory will make his disciples unspeakably happy. The plan devised and adopted for the redemption of men will appear to be the result of infinite wisdom and benevolence.

The text is descriptive of the most important part of the work the Son of God has performed, and has engaged to perform for the salvation of His people.

Its two clauses require separate and careful consideration.

I. *He shall see of the travail of His soul.*

This language is expressive of strong and very deep feelings, such as none experience except those who have been born of the Holy Spirit.

The travail of soul the Son of God experienced was not occasioned merely or chiefly by the treatment He received from His enemies before, and at the time of His crucifixion. Though born in a manger, and though He had not where to lay His head, yet He never was heard to complain of His poverty. Though rich, He voluntarily became poor, that we through His poverty might be made rich. The glory He had with His Father before the world was, He concealed in His human nature. Though at any time he could by asking, obtain from His Father more than twelve legions of angels for His protection; yet He permitted His enemies to act out toward Him the feelings of their hearts. When upon the cross His prayer was, "Father, forgive them, for they know not what they do." The travail of His soul was not occasioned by any bodily pains and sufferings. Such, indeed, is the connexion between soul and body, that the wounds and pains of the latter more or less affect the former. Those sufferings which originate in the mind are more intolerable than those which originate in the body. The travail of soul which the Son of God experienced, was internal. It admits of no adequate description, and is very imperfectly understood by the most intelligent and devoted Christian. It is a subject on which we ought intensely to meditate. No subject is better suited to move the affections of the heart, and to fasten them on Him, who is the chief among ten thousand, and altogether lovely.

In the following discourse I shall mention some of these considerations which occasioned that travail of soul, which the Son of God endured when effecting the redemption of His people.

1. His love of His Father was infinite and infinitely intense. (Its object is infinitely glorious.) Just in proportion to the strength of His love (of His Father) was His grief, on account of the disobedience and rebellion of the human race. They are His creatures, the subjects of His moral government, and dependent on God for protection and every enjoyment. The great things done for them aggravated their guilt. Man was originally made in the image of God, but little lower than the angels; like His Creator in holiness, only infinitely inferior. God crowned him with glory and honor—gave him dominion over the works of His hands, and put all things under his feet. He was made capable of holding communion with God, and was permitted to dwell near Him. It would have been a grief to the Son of God to see the image of His Father defaced and lost in all the human race. It must have been grief to the Son of God to see that law, which is holy, just, and good, and which is a transcript of the moral perfections of his Father, disregarded and trodden under foot. Every act of disobedience proceeds from opposition to the holy character of God. By the apostasy of our first parents, the whole human family, made to worship and enjoy God, became his open enemies, and by their conduct bid defiance to their rightful Sovereign. The Son of God could not see the only subjects of His Father's moral government in this world, rise up in rebellion against Him without grief, and without an earnest desire to bring them to repentance.

2. The apostasy of man did not change his relation to God as his Creator and rightful Sovereign. He sustains a nearer relation to God than children sustain to their parents. Though God was angry with him on account of his disobedience, yet He loved him as one of His creatures. "For God so loved

the world, that He gave His only begotten Son that whosoever believeth in Him might not perish, but have everlasting life." In proportion to His love of lost man was His desire of their salvation, and of His willingness to make sacrifices to effect the object. The nearer the relation we sustain to any, the more deeply are we distressed when they suffer, and especially, when by some wicked and disgraceful act they have exposed themselves to a capital punishment, which will be the punishment of every one who is not saved. How indescribable must be the agony of a fond parent, when he sees a beloved child for some great crime led away to the place of execution! How deep then must have been the distress of the Son of God, when He saw the world lying in wickedness, and all mankind exposed to everlasting death! They were, let it be remembered, more nearly related to Him than children to their parents.

The deluge and other calamities, intended to bring men to repentance, and to keep them from sinning, did not produce the intended effect. Had they repented, their repentance would not have made satisfaction for past transgression. Perfect obedience would have been demanded of them had they never sinned. The demands of the divine law must be satisfied, otherwise no transgressor can be justified. As it was impossible for the disobedient to satisfy divine justice, so they could not hope for salvation without the interposition of a proper substitute. The Son of God was the only person who could be a proper substitute: and whose perfect righteousness could be a proper foundation for the justification of the ungodly. Holy angels can do no more than discharge the duties they owe to God. They can merit nothing for their fellow-creatures. The Son of God saw millions and hundreds of millions whom He desired to save, under sentence of death, and exposed to everlasting ruin. The work to be done He saw was great. Great as it was, He was able and willing to accomplish it.

III. The apostasy of man afforded the Son of God an opportunity to do more for the honor and glory of His Father, than could have been done by the perfect obedience of all mankind. Such was the magnitude of the work he undertook to accomplish, as to require the exercise of all His powers. "And I looked, saith the Lord, And there was none to help, and I wondered that there was none to uphold, therefore mine own arm brought salvation unto me, and my fury it upheld me." (Isa. lxiii. 9.) None but a Divine person could have any adequate knowledge of the claims of an infinite God " whose kingdom is an everlasting kingdom, and whose dominion is throughout all generations." The work to be accomplished, and the means to be employed must correspond with the infinite excellence and magnitude of the object sought. All the subjects of God's moral government in all parts of His vast empire, are, or will be, more or less effected by what is done in this world. *Holy* angels, who saw some of their companions banished from heaven for their disobedience, could not adore and praise God with all their heart, unless satisfied with the plan adopted for the redemption of man. Those who are suffering the wrath of God, could not feel that their punishment is *just*, if they saw any saved in their sins, or saved without as strong an expression *as their punishment*, of God's hatred of sin.

The work of redemption must be so perfect that neither holy nor unholy angels can discover any defect in it. How difficult the work, how infinite the responsibility of the Son of God! None but a person possessed of infinite attributes could attempt to accomplish it. No man, however penitent, could without reserve trust in any other.

The humiliation of the Son of God, without which our redemption could not be accomplished, was infinite. In this we have the clearest views of the intensity of His love. To execute His purpose He must descend from His lofty height—hide His glory in humanity—humanity degraded by the apostasy, and must suffer His enemies to accuse, revile, mock Him, and put Him to the most disgraceful death. Though He was in the form of God, and thought it not robbery to be equal with God; "He made Himself of no reputation, and took upon Him the form of a servant, and was made in the likeness of men, and being found in fashion as a man, He humbled Himself and became obedient unto death, even the death of the cross." (Phil. ii. 6-8.) The humiliation of the Son of God was wonderful. When we meditate on it we are soon lost in wonder. Who of the greatest patriots or philanthropists the world ever produced, ever submitted to any humiliation like this to rescue the suffering from impending ruin? Men may have made great sacrifices, and given large sums for the promotion of some important object, they may have exposed their lives in the defence of their country; but in doing this they do not fail of obtaining the praise of men. It is much less difficult for a proud and an ambitious man to give his property and to expose his life to danger in an honorable cause, than to do that, however excellent his motives, which must expose him to reproach and contempt. It was the intense love of men, and His desire of their salvation, which moved the Son of God to make Himself of no reputation that He might accomplish His purpose. The proud and ambitious of this world always endeavor to avoid what is below their station, or what may make them less esteemed by the world. The professed piety of that man can be of no real value, which will allow him to do nothing for the cause of his Redeemer, which will not secure for him the praise of men. Fidelity in the service of Christ—that fidelity which is usually blessed to the conversion of sinners, always has exposed and always will expose the christian to reproach. "But woe unto you," said our Lord to His disciples, "when all men speak well of you, for so did their fathers to the false prophets." (Luke vi. 26.) It requires no humiliation or self-denial to occupy an important station and to do nothing which worldly men disapprove. So long as the heart of any one remains in its natural state, it must feel opposed to clear exhibitions of the character of Christ necessary to conversion.

The Son of God in the accomplishment of His work, met with strong opposition from men and from the wicked one. He had but just became incarnate, when his life was sought by Herod, king of the Jews. John, sent to prepare the way for Him, was beheaded. Innumerable invisible and evil spirits no doubt operated on the hearts of men to prevent them from receiving the truth. They are still active in opposing the work of the Son of God. They suggest objections to the essential doctrines of christianity, and furnish the impenitent with excuses for their delay of repentance. Few are aware how they are influenced by the great enemy of God and of their souls.

4. Before the Son of God could plead successfully for the pardon and justification of any of the human race, it was necessary for Him to stand in the place of sinners before their offended Sovereign, and to receive the chastisement they deserved. There is something terrible in the anger of a holy God, of which none have any conception except those who have been the subjects of the operation of the Spirit. When

the Son of God stood in the room of sinners, His Father hid His face from Him. Then His sufferings were greater than they were in the garden of Gethsemane, where He sweat as it were great drops of blood falling down to the ground. In the latter place He could adopt the language of the Son, and say, "O, my Father, if it be possible, let this cup pass from me, nevertheless not as I will, but as thou wilt." But when upon the cross and His Father's face was hidden from Him, He could not say "O, my Father," as He had done. He could only say in His extremity, "My God, my God, why hast thou forsaken me?"

Indescribable and inconceivable was the travail of soul which the Son of God experienced in effecting the salvation of His people. When He had magnified the Divine law and made it honorable by His obedience and death, He had a firm foundation on which He could rest his plea for the redemption of all given to Him in the covenant of redemption. He had done more to honor the law of God than could have been done by man, had he never sinned. His Father could not refuse to give Him a reward for the work He had performed. "All that the Father giveth me," he said, "shall come to me; and him that cometh to me, I will in no wise cast out. For I came down from heaven not to do mine own will, but the will of Him that sent me. And this is the Father's will that sent me that of all which He hath given me I should lose nothing, but should raise it up again at the last day." (John vi. 37–39.) Many as a fact have been redeemed by Him, and many are the promises that His followers shall be numerous as the stars of heaven, and as the sands upon the sea-shore. "He shall have the heathen for His inheritance, and the uttermost part of the earth for His possession." "I beheld," said John, in a vision, "and lo, a great multitude which no man could number, of all nations, and kindreds, and people, and tongues stood before the throne, and before the Lamb, clothed with white robes, and palms in their hands, and cried with a loud voice, saying, Salvation unto our God, which sitteth upon the throne, and unto the Lamb." (Rev. vii. 9, 10.)

II. The second clause of the text will next demand our attention.

The following, no doubt, are some of the considerations which will give satisfaction to the Son of God for the part He has performed in the work of redemption.

1. When the Son of God reviews the work undertaken by Him, and finds no defect in any part, nothing omitted, overlooked or imperfectly executed, He must in this particular be satisfied. It was in certain expectation of the completion of His work, that He said just before He bowed His head and gave up the ghost, "It is finished." He is the only person who could ever say this. Those christians who have made the greatest attainments in holiness, see most of their own defects, and at the close of life feel that they can depend on nothing but the righteousness of Christ. They have the most abasing views of themselves, and feel that their life has by no means corresponded with their obligations to Him who gave His life for them. They are satisfied with the method God has adopted for their redemption. They discover no defect in it. The more they meditate on it the more they are satisfied that it is the result of infinite wisdom and benevolence. It is as honorable to God as it is safe for men. God can be just—appear righteous to all the subjects of his moral government, and the justifier of him that believeth in Jesus. *The plan and work of redemption gives us brighter views of the glorious per-*

fections of God, than could have been given by the moral law. The satisfaction of the believer is wholly derived from his union with Christ, of whose joy and glory he is made a partaker, Christ is just such a Saviour as he needs, and appears to be altogether lovely and glorious.

2. The success which results from the completion of the part assigned to the Son of God in the work of redemption, must afford Him satisfaction. With what delight must he, after his ascension, have looked down upon Jerusalem, near which city He was crucified, when He saw in one day, three thousand converted and numbered with the disciples? Holy angels also were delighted to see Him whom they worshiped, so highly honored. There is joy in heaven, in their presence, over one sinner that repenteth; how great must be their joy when God revives His work and many are converted!

Nothing affords greater satisfaction to men than the success which attends any enterprise in which they may be engaged. The degree of satisfaction they experience corresponds with its importance, and the obstacles overcome.

The work performed by the Son of God was the most important and difficult ever undertaken, infinitely above the powers of any created being, or of all created beings united. Indeed it was more difficult and important than the work of creation. In the work of creation there was no obstacle to overcome; but in the work of redemption, the enmity of the human heart and the mighty power of wicked angels must be overcome. The work of creation makes no exhibition of the forgiving love of God; but in the work of redemption we have the brightest view of the glory of God.

In every instance, the plan of redemption, when cordially approved, has produced its legitimate result. "Him that cometh unto me," said Christ, "I will in no wise cast out." No one can ever say that he trusted in Christ, and did not obtain the pardon of his sins and the hope of future life and happiness. If any perish, it will not be because the work performed by the Son of God is in any part imperfect, but because they refuse to trust in Him. It is unreasonable to condemn the remedy prescribed for a disease, by those who refuse to receive it, especially when they have the most abundant proofs that all who have made use of it have been effectually cured. The Son of God may well be satisfied with what He has done, as every one has obtained a good hope of salvation who has accepted of His offer, and put their trust in Him. His righteousness is as sufficient for all mankind as for a single individual.

3. Christianity, whenever known and *externally respected*, has produced the most beneficial effects. Every missionary station established but a few years in a pagan land, affords a proof of this. The wilderness and the solitary place is made glad for them, and the desert is made to rejoice and blossom as the rose. The eyes of the blind are opened, the ears of the deaf are unstopped. "The lame man is made to leap as a hart, and the tongue of the dumb to sing; for in the wilderness waters break out, and streams in the desert."

What crime can be named which christianity does not condemn? It urges, by the most powerful motives, strict obedience to all the precepts of the moral law. Should the moral law be carefully observed, even among us, we should witness a happy change in the state of society even in this christian country; and how much greater in a pagan country? With respect to temporal comforts and privileges, there is a great difference between pagan and christian countries, and between those countries where the Gospel in its simplicity is received, and where a corrupt system has influence. None of the evils which exist in christian countries can be traced to the principles of christianity as the direct cause. Christianity is opposed to the corrupt opinions and practices of men. On this account it meets with opposition more or less violent. The fault is not in Christianity, but in those who oppose it, and zealously contend against its holy doctrines.

4. Another consideration gives satisfaction to Christ. He had the unqualified approbation of His Father. His resurrection from the dead was a miracle performed by His Father, and had reference to all that He had done, and was a proof that His Father fully approved the work He had finished. The descent of the Holy Spirit was another proof that His work was approved.

The Holy Spirit is never sent to accompany or to give success to error—to any opinion or system dishonorable to the character or government of God. To have the approbation of His Father was the greatest reward the Son of God desired. His Father gave Him a seat at His right hand. This was conferring the highest honor upon Him for what He had done. What more could He desire? What more could His friends desire for Him?

The prayers offered by the Son of God being always offered in submission to His Father's will, were always answered. "*I came down from heaven,*" he said, "*not to do mine own will, but the will of Him that sent me.* And this is the Father's will which hath sent me, that of all which He hath given me I should lose nothing, but should raise it up again at the last day. And this is the will of Him that sent me, that every one which seeth the Son and believeth on Him, may have everlasting life: and I will raise him up at the last day." (John vi. 38–40.) His reward will correspond with the promises of His Father. All revivals of religion, and all conversions are granted in answer to His prayers, and in fulfilment of promises made Him. It is in answer to His prayers that the Holy Spirit, the Comforter, is sent to visit the churches and to enable them to offer those prayers for the conversion of sinners, which God never fails to answer. It is the Holy Spirit, the third person in the ever blessed Trinity, by whom sinners are awakened, convicted, converted, and vitally united to Christ. By the same agent they are sanctified and prepared for admittance into heaven.

APPLICATION.

1. The subject of this discourse furnishes christians with a standard by which they may form a correct judgment respecting their prayers and lives. "If any man have not the spirit of Christ," said the apostle, "he is none of His." God is ever ready to hear the prayers of His church when offered with deep and right feelings of heart—indeed when they correspond but imperfectly with the prayers of Christ. How can they expect their prayers to be heard, if they do not proceed from their heart? "Ye hypocrites!" said Christ, to the Scribes and Pharisees, "well did Esaias prophesy of you, saying, This people draweth nigh unto me with their mouths, and honoreth me with their lips, but their heart is far from me." (Matt. xv. 7, 8.) That prayer which does not proceed from the heart, cannot be accepted. It is an offence to God. It seems to be an attempt to deceive the omniscient and heart-searching God. Men of the world cannot be persuaded that those whose hearts appear to be unaffected when they pray, can believe

the doctrines they profess to believe, or which they teach. How can any christian freely believe that all who have not been born of the Holy Spirit are under sentence of death, and be unmoved when offering prayer for their conversion? It is not sufficient to offer words, however beautiful the expressions, if they do not proceed from the heart. What the Son of God did for the salvation of men corresponded with the travail of His soul. Though rich, He became poor. He exposed Himself by His faithful exhibitions of the truth, to reproach, scorn, persecution and death. It is impossible for those who give grudgingly of their substance for the cause of their Redeemer, and who, to obtain the praise of men, conceal or modify the most essential doctrines of the Gospel, to experience any travail of soul when praying for the conversion of sinners.

2. How few prayers are offered with the unction of the Spirit! Ardent love of God and of the souls of men, if accompanied by corresponding labors, will move the hearts of christians to offer acceptable prayers to God for the conversion of sinners. God is more ready to grant the Holy Spirit than we are with proper feelings to ask for this great blessing. "And it shall come to pass," saith the Lord, "that before they call I will answer, and while they are yet speaking I will hear." (Isaiah lxv. 24.) Enlarged views of the character of God, the worth of the soul, the deep depravity of the human heart, and the value of the price paid for the redemption of men, can hardly fail to draw forth the agonizing prayer of the church for the effusions of the Holy Spirit, by whose power sinners may be saved and become the followers of Christ. Men of the world judge correctly whether prayers proceed from the heart, or are only the service of the lips. The mere outward performance of duty strengthens the unbelief of sin-

ners, and, if long continued, makes them unwilling to receive those truths which God makes effectual to the salvation of sinners.

3. Christians, when they compare their lives with the standard exhibited to view in this discourse, can never be satisfied with themselves; but may be satisfied with the foundation of their hope. If we say that we are perfect, that will prove us perverse. The more eminent any are for piety, the more clearly the light of the Holy Spirit shines in their souls, and the more they discover of the depths of human depravity.

The satisfaction of believers must be derived from their union with Christ, in whom there is an infinite fulness. If the Son of God who did so much for the redemption of men, and who gave the most undeniable proofs of His love of His Father and of the world, can be satisfied, all who are united to Him must be satisfied, and must partake of His joy. But why so few are saved, and why so many millions of the human race remain ignorant of the Gospel, we know not. When the Son of God finished His work on the earth, He said to His disciples, the apostles, "Go ye into all the world, and preach the Gospel to every creature. He that believeth and is baptized, shall be saved; but he that believeth not shall be damned." Here we have a proof of His unbounded liberality. He is no respecter of persons, is as ready to save the poor as the rich. Why God did not prevent the angels that fell from sinning, we know not. And why He does not, by the mighty power of His Spirit, convert whole congregations where the Gospel is *faithfully* preached, we know not. If it be not inconsistent with His infinite goodness that men suffer in this world, it may not be if they suffer in the future world. The fact is made known that the angels that sinned are "reserved in chains under darkness, unto the judgment of the great day." They are as dear to God as His creatures, as any impenitent of the human race. Let not any persuade themselves that God will not punish them if they refuse to accept the offer freely made of salvation through faith in Christ. God will not change His purpose, but will do as He has said. Be persuaded, sinner, to seek refuge in Christ while you have opportunity. And may God bless the word which you have heard. Amen.

CHRIST, AND HIM CRUCIFIED.

1 CORINTHIANS II. 2.

"For I determined not to know anything among you save Jesus Christ, and Him crucified."

THE passage of Scripture from which the text has been taken, is descriptive of the manner in which Paul, the most thoroughly educated, laborious and successful of all the apostles, preached the Gospel at Corinth, one of the most opulent, splendid and polished of the cities of Greece—a city which abounded with renowned philosophers, accomplished orators, and other learned men. The chief topic of his conversation, and constant theme of his discourses in that gay, corrupt, and idolatrous city, was the redemption of man through faith in Jesus Christ, and Him crucified.

The great and wonderful change the apostle had experienced in his own views and feelings, which had been produced by the mighty power of God, and his cordial reception of the truths of the Gospel, gave a new direction to his thoughts and pursuits, and made him, who had been a most determined enemy of christianity, one of its warmest and firmest friends. The more perfectly he understood the method God had devised and adopted for the redemption of lost men, the more freely he was convinced that it was the result of infinite wisdom and benevolence. It appeared to him to be exactly suited to the wants of all classes of the human race. He discovered in it no defect, and nothing superfluous. He felt that any attempt at embellishment, like clouds before the sun, would only obscure its glory, diminish its influence, and divert the attention of his hearers from those considerations which most deeply concerned them. He also felt that christianity does not need any system of philosophy which is the offspring of human reason, to render it acceptable to men, and to increase its influence. It is itself the most perfect system of heavenly philosophy, of which God Himself is the author.

When exhibited in its simplicity it makes the most powerful, lasting and salutary impressions on the minds of men, and produces the most happy results.

Nothing has done so much to corrupt christianity, and to render its distinguishing doctrines powerless, as endeavors to accelerate its progress by uniting it with some system of philosophy. That the apostle had this view of the subject, is manifest from the following passage in his epistle to the Colossians: "Beware lest any man spoil you through philosophy and vain deceit, after the tradition of men, after the rudiments of the world, and not after Christ. For in Him dwelleth all the fullness of the Godhead bodily." (Col. ii. 8, 9.)

There have been some in every age, who, relying more on the powers of their mind or on the perfection of human instrumentality than on the mighty energy of the Holy Spirit, have persuaded themselves that those doctrines of the Gospel to which the unrenewed are most opposed, can be so explained as to appear reasonable to the intelligent members of society, and worthy of their cordial approbation. If this can be done, the work of the Holy Spirit must be unnecessary. The infidel does not object to opinions and doctrines which appear to him to be agreeable to the principles and laws of human reason. How then, he may be asked, can he account for the fact that Christ, the most perfect teacher in the world, and who "spake as never man spake," met with the most violent opposition of the most intelligent of the Jews?

By the accommodation of christianity to human reason, the most pernicious errors have been introduced into the church, and have at different periods prevailed. It is difficult for men of strong powers of mind, and of extensive learning, who are admired for their pleasing manners and their eloquence, to depend for success on the word and Spirit of God. The applause they receive not only begets a love of praise, but also a desire so to modify the most unpopular doctrines, as to enable them to preach them without giving offence. Hence we seldom find a very popular preacher a bold advocate of the distinguishing truths of christianity. Some, with a view to increase the number of their converts, do modify those truths to which the unrenewed are most opposed. It is easier to do this than to humble themselves before God, and by impartial self-examination, intense meditation on the truth, and persevering prayer to seek for the Holy Spirit.

It was the aim of the apostle to preach the Gospel in its greatest simplicity, that its fruits might be genuine. In this way he looked for sound conversions and great success. "And I, brethren," he said to the church, at Corinth, where his success was great, "when I came to you, I came not with excellency of speech or of wisdom, declaring unto you the testimony of God, and my speech and my preaching was not with enticing words of man's wisdom, but in the demonstration of spirit and of power." The reason is given. "That your faith should not stand in the wisdom of men, but in the power of God"—in other words that your faith should not be the result of moral suasion, but the effect of the mighty power of God.

(1 Cor. ii. 1–5.) Christianity, when divested of everything not essential to it, gives us the clearest view of the character of God, and the changes produced by it are the most satisfactory.

Paul, the greatest and most successful of all the apostles, when filled with the Holy Ghost, and meditating on the redemption of lost men, through faith in Jesus Christ, and him crucified, was so overpowered with a view—1, of the *grandeur and comprehensiveness of the plan adopted for its accomplishment—2, its relation to us, and its perfect adaptation to the wants of all classes of men—3, and its perpetually unfolding wonders that he could think and speak of nothing else.*

To these particulars suggested for our consideration by the text, your attention in the following discourse will be directed.

I. The grandeur and comprehensiveness of the plan of redemption.

1. The grandeur and comprehensiveness of the plan of redemption appear from the following considerations: God is its author; it reveals and equally interests the three persons in the ever blessed Trinity, its influence extends to all worlds, to all ages, distinguishes lost men from lost angels, exhibits to view the wonderful union of the mercy and justice of God in the deliverance of all who believe in Jesus Christ and him crucified, from the deepest degradation and wretchedness, and in their restoration to the favor of their offended Sovereign. Holy angels, great in dignity, in knowledge and wisdom, desire to look into these things, and delight to worship the Son of God, and to minister to his disciples. Christianity is "the power of God, and the wisdom of God to every one that believeth."

More than twenty years after, Paul, the most laborious and

successful of the apostles, though favored with the teachings of the Holy Spirit, felt that his knowledge of the forgiving love of God was extremely limited. "Brethren," he said, in his epistle to the Philippians, "I count not myself to have apprehended; but this one thing I do: forgetting those things that are behind, and reaching forth unto those things that are before, I press toward the mark for the prize of the high calling of God in Christ Jesus."

2. The end which God has in view, and which he is pursuing in all his works, is another and most important consideration. All the revelations of God make it manifest that the glory of his holiness is the *ultimate end* he has in view in his works of creation and providence, and more especially in his work of redemption. When he created the world, the morning stars who were spectators of the grand exhibition of power, and wisdom, and goodness, "sang together, and all the sons of God shouted for joy." How great must have been their wonder, delight and rapture, when the purpose of God to redeem ruined men, was made known to them! Though a different order of intelligent beings, they feel interested in the welfare of the human race. The repentance of one sinner, however obscure his situation, and however lightly he may be esteemed by his fellow-creatures, is an event of such magnitude, as to occasion joy in the presence of the angels of God. But their attention is not directed exclusively to the happiness of the redeemed; their thoughts dwell on the wonders of the forgiving love of God.

3. This world, dark as it is by reason of the apostasy of the human race, by the forgiving love of God here revealed, is made the brightest light in the universe, inconceivably brighter than the natural sun, shining with meridian splendor. It

increases the light of heaven, and makes the darkness in which the wicked dwell more terrible.

The glory of God's holiness is a higher and nobler end than the happiness of the universe. This was the end he had in view before he commenced the work of creation. Men of the noblest feelings will sooner sacrifice their lives than their honor. The true christian will sooner submit to persecution, to the loss of his property and life than his good name. Many have been brought to the trial, and have chosen rather to suffer a martyr's death than to do anything inconsistent with their christian character.

4. There is a grandeur and comprehensiveness in the *means* employed for the redemption of men.

When it appeared in the counsels of heaven that no created being could accomplish the work of redemption, the Son of God, the second person in the ever blessed Trinity, and of equal dignity with his Father, offered to undertake it and his offer was accepted. "For God so loved the world that he gave his only begotten Son, that whosoever believeth in him should not perish, but have everlasting life. For God sent not his Son into the world to condemn the world; but that the world through him might be saved." (John iii. 16, 17.) The Son of God had in view the glory of his Father, the support of his government, and its influence on holy angels, and those too who apostatized, and on the millions and hundreds of millions of the human race. He knew how he should be treated by those whose salvation was near his heart. Though glorious in holiness, and infinitely happy, yet he so tenderly regarded the honor of his Father, and so intense was his love of the human race, that he left the most delightful place in the universe, divested himself of the glory he had with his Father before the foundation of the world, assumed human nature, that he might by his obedience and death satisfy the demands of the Divine law, and effect the redemption of all who might trust in him.

When he commenced his journey to this rebellious province of his Father's empire, the object to be accomplished was so glorious, that a great company of holy angels attended him, as ministering spirits, desirous of being near him, that they might behold his wonderful works. An angel announced his birth, "and suddenly there was with the angel a multitude of the heavenly host praising God, and saying, Glory to God in the highest, and on earth peace and good will toward men." (Luke ii. 14.)

The attention of holy angels and wicked spirits is constantly directed to the habitations of men, where God performs his works of grace, the former to minister to the church, and the latter to corrupt, divide and trouble the professed friends of God.

The Son of God being a Divine person, is not the Saviour of a particular nation, but he is the Saviour and light of the world. The law which he magnified and made honorable by his obedience and death, extends to all mankind. His righteousness is sufficient for the whole human race. No one will perish because there is not room enough in heaven for him, nor because there is any defect in the atonement made by Jesus Christ. Great beyond description is the work Christ has performed, and great beyond conception were the sufferings he endured for the redemption of men. This interposition for lost men is the wonder of holy angels, and of wicked spirits. It delights the former but distresses the latter. It is and ever will be the wonder of saints on earth, and saints in heaven.

While in this imperfect state, our views of the glory of God in the redemption of men are exceedingly obscure and circumscribed. "We see spiritual things through a glass darkly." "Now I know in part," said the apostle, "but then (referring to a future state) shall I know even as I am known." God makes such revelations of himself as are necessary for us, and as in our weakness we are able to bear. Were he now to give us such a view of his glory as we shall have hereafter, we should be overpowered. When Moses besought the Lord to show him his glory, he did not, probably, correctly understand the import of his request. "And God said, I will make all my goodness pass before thee, and I will be gracious to whom I will be gracious, and I will show mercy on whom I will show mercy. And he said, Thou canst not see my face; for there shall no man see me and live. And the Lord said, There is a place by me, and thou shalt stand upon a rock: and it shall come to pass, while my glory passeth by, that I will put thee in the cleft of the rock, and will cover thee with my hand while I pass by; and I will take away my hand, and thou shalt see my back parts, but my face shall not be seen." (Ex. xxxiii. 19–23.) Great objects and boundless scenes are constantly passing before the mind of the devout christian, compared with which the objects and scenes of this world appear to be hardly worthy of notice. Nothing so enlarges the mind and elevates the thoughts as the contemplation of the work of redemption.

The work of redemption is as much more magnificent and glorious than the work of creation, as the perfections of God are more fully and gloriously displayed in the former than in the latter. The price paid for our redemption is of more value than all the gold and silver of the world. "Forasmuch as ye know," said the apostle Peter, "that ye were not redeemed with corruptible things, such as silver and gold, from your vain conversation, received by tradition from your fathers; but with the precious blood of Christ, as of a lamb without blemish and without spot." (1 Peter i. 18, 19.) When we withdraw our thoughts from the affairs of this world and fix them on him who gave his life to redeem us, the object before us appears to be infinitely great and glorious. No wonder the apostle, when his attention was directed to it, could think and speak of nothing else. Nothing else when compared with it, appeared to be worthy of his notice. "But what things were gain to me," he said, "I counted loss for Christ; yea, doubtless, I count all things but loss for the excellency of the knowledge of Christ Jesus, my Lord, for whom I have suffered the loss of all things, and do count them of no value that I may win Christ." (Phil. iii. 8, 9.)

5. By the death of Christ, our substitute, who was Himself holy, harmless, undefiled, and separate from sinners, and made higher than the heavens, we obtain the most correct knowledge of our demerit as transgressors of the divine law. Had not sinful man deserved death, God would not have permitted His dearly beloved Son to die in His stead. None can be saved through faith in Jesus Christ, and him crucified, who do not understand and feel that they deserve death.

As Christ was God manifest in the flesh, the feelings expressed toward him were expressed toward God. Can it be doubted that those who crucified Him, would, had they possessed the power, have subverted the government, and destroyed the life of his Father? Had the Jews been convinced that Jesus of Nazareth is the true Messiah, they might have been afraid to put him to death. But the restraints of fear would not have changed the feelings of their hearts. All who persevere in unbelief do, in their hearts, approve of the conduct of the Jews, otherwise they would unite with the followers of Christ. This disposition is discovered in the little child as soon as he has an understanding of the truths of Christianity. In the death of Christ we see united the inflexible justice and abounding mercy of God.

The redemption of man through faith in Jesus Christ, and him crucified, gives us the most affecting and transforming views of the character of God, and of the glory of His holiness. Christ, the Son of God, is declared to be the brightness of his Father's glory, and the express image of His person. By him God has made such a revelation of His forgiving love as could not be made by the moral law. There is no intimation in this law of the forgiving love of God. The visible heavens declare the glory of God's power, and wisdom and goodness; but give us no knowledge of His mercy to lost men. The language of the moral law is, "The soul that sinneth it shall die, and cursed is every one that continueth not in all things written in the book of the law to do them." The moral law is a transcript of the character of the God of nature, so far as revealed to our first parents before their apostasy. Christ is declared to be the brightness of his Father's glory, because in him are united mercy and truth, righteousness and peace. Such is the plan adopted for the redemption of men, as to give additional lustre to those attributes of God, which were displayed in the work of creation, and as to make such revelations of Himself as could not otherwise be made to intelligent, moral beings. It maintains all the rights and claims of God, and offers freely eternal life to all who believe in Christ. How rich the grace of God! How boundless His liberality! The more intensely we meditate on the doctrines peculiar to Christianity, the more precious they appear to us, and the more our hearts are affected. When we meditate only for a short time with a devotional spirit on what Christ has done for us, our hearts overflow with love to Him, and we are filled with wonder and joy unspeakable and full of glory, and while thus employed our views become enlarged, grand and sublime objects pass before our minds, and we obtain an earnest and a foretaste of that inheritance prepared for the redeemed.

No event recorded in the history of the world is so important, and which has been productive of so much good as the death of Christ. He gave his life that he might redeem lost men from the bondage and consequences of sin. In the gift of His Son to sinners, God the Father has made it manifest that He is the most compassionate Being in the universe. How unspeakable the gift of the Son of God. What can be more dear to an affectionate parent than a beloved and an only son, a son of unblemished character, and possessing every possible excellence? To give such a son to suffer, the innocent for the guilty, the just for the unjust, and to suffer an ignominious and cruel death, must be a greater proof of his love and mercy than to give all his possessions. The same spirit influenced the Son as well as the Father.

No one can read the history of God's forgiving love, and maintain that He is an unfeeling Sovereign. When His beloved Son stood in the room of sinners, He did not spare him. When upon the cross, and more than ever feeling the need of support, his Father hid His face from him, and left him to perform alone that part, without the accomplishment of which none could be saved. He could not in his extremity cry, "My Father, my Father," as he had done, but only, "My God, my

God," the cry of a malefactor in distress, "why hast thou forsaken me?"

It is the preaching of Christ, and him crucified, which gives to the hearer not only the clearest, but the only just view of the divine character. It also produces the greatest and the most excellent results. It excites no worldly hopes or fears. When a friend dies he can do nothing more for us, and when an enemy dies we can fear him no longer. When our thoughts are fastened on the death of Christ, who died, the just for the unjust, we cannot but understand and feel that we deserve death—that God will execute His law upon all impenitent transgressors, and that salvation is to be obtained only by a vital union to His Son. That submission, which is produced by selfish hopes or fears, is of no value. And unless we love the character of God on account of its own excellency, independent of any hope of future happiness, or fear of future misery, our love cannot be pure, and such as God can approve. It is not, however, meant that love of God does not always produce hope of future happiness, and deliverance from the fear of future misery. We are never so happy as when so filled with all the fullness of God as to forget ourselves, and to think of nothing but the glory of God, as it shines in the face of Jesus Christ, and him crucified.

II. The relation Jesus Christ and him crucified sustains to us and our fellow-creatures, or, the perfect adaptation of the plan of redemption to the wants of all classes of men.

Events, which interest *us*, but which others think unworthy of their notice, may so powerfully affect our minds, as to exclude from them every other subject. The death of a dear friend, a beloved child, a husband, or a wife, affects us more than the slaughter of thousands in some distant part of the world. Had the Son of God interposed for the salvation of the angels that sinned, it would be our duty to rejoice in their redemption and restoration to the favor of God. There is joy, we are assured, in the presence of the angels of God over one sinner that repenteth. They, though a different order of beings, rejoice in the happiness of the human race.

That God should pass by the angels that sinned, who once dwelt near Him, and who had faithfully served Him for an unknown period, and that He should send into this world His only begotten and dearly beloved Son to redeem an inferior order of beings, and that He should permit him to suffer death that we may live, is indeed wonderful. Surely, such distinguishing goodness to us should soften our hard hearts, and lead us to repentance. It may have been the inquiry of the angels that sinned, ever since they knew any thing of the work of redemption, Why did God pass us by and reserve us in chains under darkness unto the judgment of the great day, and exercise His forgiving love to the human race? We can give no answer to this inquiry. We can only say, Even so Father, for so it hath seemed good in thy sight. Why, too, those who have died in pagan lands—the millions and hundreds of millions who have perished without any knowledge of the way of salvation through faith in Jesus Christ, and him crucified, why, they may inquire, was not the gospel made known to us? Had the mighty works been done among us, they may say, which have been done in Christian lands, we should have repented, and been saved. While millions, and hundreds of millions remain in total darkness with respect to the redemption of men, the light of Christianity shines upon us with unclouded splendor. That God should leave so many of our fellow-creatures to perish, when an atonement has been made sufficient for all mankind, and furnish us so richly with the means of grace, is a proof of His distinguishing love.

The complete success of the scheme, which has been devised and adopted for our salvation, must interest all who regard the honor of God, their own, and the happiness of their fellow-creatures; and who compare the Christian religion with any system received in the world. Christianity is suited to every variety of case as well as person. Jesus Christ, and him crucified, sustains a near relation to all, who believe in his name. They are vitally united to him, as the branch to the vine, or the members to the body. Because He lives, they will live also. This vital union, in connexion with the promises of God, is the proper foundation of their hope of final salvation.

Great changes have been produced in individuals and in communities by the faithful preaching of the doctrines of the cross. Innumerable are the ways in which Christianity improves the condition as well as character of men. It is impossible for us to know while we are in this world how many have been, or will be saved through faith in Jesus Christ. The number of the redeemed whom John in vision saw in heaven was great. "And I beheld," said John, "and heard the voice of many angels round about the throne, and the beasts or living creatures, and the elders, and the number of them was ten thousand times ten thousand, and thousands of thousands." Since John had this vision a great multitude have been converted of our fellow-creatures, and very many of the people of this country. How immense must be the number of our fellow-creatures, who have been and will be saved, when all the promises of God are fulfilled—when the whole earth is filled with the knowledge of God as the waters cover the sea.

Should we ascend the loftiest mountain on earth, the circle bounded by the utmost limits of our vision would not be sufficient to contain them. But there is room enough in heaven, and grace enough in Christ for all, who desire salvation through faith in Him. And the command of Christ to His apostles, and through them to the church was, after his resurrection, when all national distinctions were abolished, "Go ye into all the world, and preach the gospel to every creature."

The most extensive diffusion of the light of Christianity by no means diminishes its power. It only multiplies lights, the greater the number of which, the greater is the light of the world. Christ is abundantly able to save all that come to Him; thousands and tens of thousands, as well as individuals. No one that did come was rejected.

What other physician was ever known able to heal all manner of diseases? What other philanthropist was ever able to deliver the poor and wretched from the slavery of Satan? In view of the cross of Christ we may adopt the triumphant language of the apostle: "Where is the wise? where is the scribe? where is the disputer of this world? hath not God made foolish the wisdom of this world? For after that in the wisdom of God, the world by wisdom knew not God, it pleased God by the foolishness of preaching, to save them that believe." But the foolishness of God is wiser than men, and the weakness of God is stronger than men. Greater power is displayed in the deliverance of a single individual from the bondage of sin than can be exerted by the combined forces of the whole human race. And the salvation of a single individual is a greater good than the sum of all the temporal good that ever has been, or ever will be enjoyed. The happiness of the redeemed will forever increase.

Those, supposed to be converts, who have no consistent views of Jesus Christ, and him crucified, seldom, if ever, long continue to give any satisfactory evidence of being truly reconciled to God. They may have experienced great changes —may have passed from a state of deep distress to a state of great joy; but may not be vitally united to Christ. Many changes are experienced, which are not saving. No matter how great they are, and how much joy they produce, if they do not result in a cordial union with Christ, they are deceptive, and of no value. There have been not a few, who during some modern revivals, have been pronounced converts, but who after the excitement has subsided, have manifested more opposition than ever to the distinguishing doctrines of Christianity. Unless the doctrines of the cross are made prominent in the ministry of the Word, hopes will be indulged without any radical change of heart, and revivals will be spurious. It was a view of the wonderful, happy, and permanent effects produced by the power of the Holy Ghost, operating in connection with the preaching of Christ, and him crucified, which filled the mind of the apostle with admiration of the plan devised and adopted for the redemption of men. What can produce in the heart of every one such a thrill of joy as evidence that he is vitally united to Christ, and one with him? And what so much delights pious parents as evidence that their children are truly converted to God through faith in Jesus Christ, and him crucified? The possession of great worldly riches is not to be compared with the possession of a good hope of salvation. The humblest Christian, who dwells in obscurity, but who enjoys fellowship with his Redeemer, would not exchange situations with the most opulent prince in the world, who has no good hope beyond the grave.

The distinguishing goodness of God to us, who dwell in this Christian land, where we have witnessed among our own friends and acquaintance the mighty changes produced by the operations of the Holy Spirit, is a subject on which we cannot meditate without perceiving our hearts overflow with gratitude to Him, who has brought salvation near to every one of us. And, brethren, if we have ourselves been renewed, how great must be our obligations to Him, and how intensely ought we to love Him, who has thus made us to differ from others, no more guilty and deserving of His wrath than ourselves?

III. Redemption through faith in Jesus Christ, and him crucified, is a subject which appears to be always *new* to those Christians and divines who have made the greatest attainment in holiness. It can never be exhausted. The knowledge of it which the most eminent divine obtains while in this life is very limited compared with what may be known. It is a remarkable fact that those who are most distinguished for piety, dwell most on the doctrines of the cross, and give the most satisfactory evidence that their hearts are affected. When they pray, exhort, or reprove, they speak from their heart. The piety is of a doubtful character of those preachers who dwell almost exclusively on the attributes and government of God, the God of nature, and seldom make the doctrines of the cross the subjects of their meditations and discourses.

Those divines most distinguished for their talents, learning, and knowledge of the Scriptures, at the close of a long life devoted to the service of God, have not hesitated to acknowledge that they have never ceased to discover new beauties in the character of their Redeemer, and in the plan adopted for our deliverance from the power of sin, and restoration to the favor of God. As the work of sanctification progresses, and they pass from one degree of grace to another, new views of the plan and work of redemption are presented to their minds, and new fields of contemplation are discovered. The time will never come, while we are in this world, and the point in duration will never be reached in eternity, when we shall know all that may be known of the redemption of men through faith in Jesus Christ. How limited, then, must be the knowledge acquired in this life, compared with the attainments which will be made in the future state!

Much sin remains in the heart of every Christian, which darkens his understanding, and exposes him to the influence of errors, which appear to favor the rapid progress of the church. The great apostle of the Gentiles not far probably from twenty years after his conversion did not hesitate to confess that he had still to struggle with indwelling sin. "For that which I do," he said, "I allow not: for what I would that I do not; but what I hate that do I. For the good that I would I do not; but the evil which I would not, that I do." (Rom. vii. 15, 19.)

Though there is some variety in the intellectual powers of men—some variety in their education, and in the circumstances of their life, as there is no change in the word and Spirit of God, the leading features of their religious experience must be the same. The experience of every Christian seems to be a series of conversions. Every new change enlarges his views of the plan and work of redemption, and gives him deeper views of the demerit of sin, and of the depravity of his heart. In passing from one degree of grace to another, it seems to the Christian that his past attainments are of but little value.

Scientific men, possessed of strong powers of mind and of extensive learning, after pursuing their studies with great diligence for many years, are ready to confess that the field of investigation appears to be wider than ever. Indeed, it is impossible during the longest life to learn all that may be known of the works of creation. Every successive year furnishes some new chapter in the history of the works of creation. The philosopher and the naturalist are constantly discovering novelties in the productions of nature. The laws of nature, and their various combinations are very imperfectly understood.

But the work of redemption far exceeds the work of creation in grandeur and comprehensiveness of design, mode of accomplishment, and excellence of results. The objects of this visible world are insignificant, compared with those which will rise before us, when eternal scenes will be disclosed.

No two chapters, either in the history of the church of God or in the history of any nation, are exactly alike. As the circumstances which affect the operations of any church vary in different periods, and in different countries, so we obtain new views of the work of grace, and of the movements of Christians every successive year. The labors of the church and the works of the Holy Spirit are new every day. Holy angels are constantly observing all our conduct, and feel interested in every new case of repentance. They are no doubt delighted when they witness the display of God's power in reviving His work, and in making additions to the number of the followers of His beloved Son.

When Christians are most thoroughly roused from their slumbers; when all their powers are exercised to the highest degree, and they meditate most intensely on the forgiving love of God, manifested through faith in Jesus Christ and him crucified, then they most rapidly increase in knowledge—then new wonders in quick succession pass before them. When professing Christians discover nothing new in the volume of revelation, and the Scriptures cease to interest them, the evidence is strong, either that they are not what they profess to be, or that they have neglected those duties, on the faithful performance of which depends their growth in grace. Unless the Scriptures appear to those who minister in holy things, to possess the charms of holy and spiritual novelty, their discourses will be uninteresting, and their prayers will be heartless.

When men of intelligence have read once or twice the publications of the most celebrated and learned authors, they lay them aside as no longer interesting from their novelty. It is far otherwise with that Book, of which God is the author. It is itself a library, containing an inexhaustible fund of the most precious truths. While diligently studying the Scriptures, new thoughts are constantly suggested to the mind, which fill it with delight and rapture. When the redemption of men through faith in Jesus Christ, and him crucified is the subject of our meditations, the field of contemplation appears to be boundless—the farther we proceed in it the more magnificent are the objects we behold—the more sublime the scenes which pass before us, the more holy and elevated are our affections, the more ardent our desires, the more honorable our purposes, the higher our joys, and the more completely our souls are filled with all the fullness of God.

REFLECTIONS.

From the view we have taken of the subject under consideration it is manifest that the truths peculiar to Christianity ought to be made prominent in the discourses of every preacher, and also in the meditations of every hearer. They ought to occupy the thoughts of every one who is anxious to obtain salvation.

Few are perhaps aware that a man may preach many years, be very eloquent, operate powerfully on the feelings of his hearers, take his subjects from the Scriptures, and even from the New Testament, and may not express a sentiment to which the Pelagian, the Unitarian or infidel can have any objection.

The serious infidel can have no objection to discourses on the natural attributes of God—his power, wisdom, goodness, omnipresence, and immutability. He can have no objection to discourses on the providence of God, or on His government, if Christianity occupy no place in it. He can have no objection to discourses on the precepts of the moral law, which is the law of nature, written in the hearts of all men, and discoverable by the light of reason. This law extends through the whole volume of revelation. Christianity contains it; but the latter does not contain the former. The infidel may admit that men are sinners, and as life is uncertain, that they ought to repent immediately. When meditating on the condition of great transgressors, his sympathies may be excited, he may endeavor to alarm them by dwelling on the penalty of the Divine law, and may with power of argument urge them without delay to submit to God. This the infidel may do, and not even mention the doctrine of justification by faith in Jesus Christ, and him crucified.

He may dwell on the reasonableness of the duties he urges his hearers to perform, making this, their reasonableness, and not the command or testimony of God, the ground of their obligation. Not a few contend that they are not under obligation to receive any doctrine unless it can be made to appear to them reasonable. They do not admit the depravity of their heart, which must be renewed, otherwise the doctrines peculiar to Christianity will never appear to be agreeable to their reason. Their reason may be exercised in ascertaining what God has revealed, and in receiving his testimony. But the things of the Spirit are foolishness to the unrenewed. If the doctrines of Christianity can be so explained as to appear reasonable to the unrenewed, they cannot need any radical change.

Many subjects may be taken from the New Testament, which relate to the perfect example of Christ, which are moral; and beautiful discourses may be delivered, abounding with elegant extracts from the published writings of men of genius, without admitting the necessity of the imputed righteousness of Christ as the only foundation of a good hope of salvation. Who that has any respect for sacred history will deny that there was such a person in Judea as Jesus Christ—that he was born at the time and place mentioned—that he performed many wonderful works--that he sustained an unblemished character, and that he suffered death on the cross? Many facts interwoven with the history of his nativity—his ministry—his sufferings, and his resurrection, the Unitarian or infidel may admit. But the infidel and Unitarian believe that he was a mere man, like Plato or Socrates, or any other distinguished moralist. They believe that his death was that of a martyr.

There are some general views of the decrees and sovereignty of God, to which neither infidels nor Unitarians can have any objection. No people more firmly believe than the Mahometans the doctrine of predestination. Around us are many illustrations of Divine sovereignty. We see one rich, another poor—one sick, another in the enjoyment of health—one dies in youth, another in the midst of life, and another lives to a good old age. The ship of one merchant returns with a valuable cargo, that of another is lost. The general doctrine of election is only a branch or particular view of the doctrine of Divine decrees. It is no proof that a man is a Christian because he believes or preaches these doctrines.

A man may be an infidel at heart, and may so preach as to be instrumental of producing a great excitement—may persuade many to submit to God, and may acquire the reputation of a great revival preacher. It is one thing to submit to God as a Being of superior power, and another to submit to Him as a Being of infinite holiness and excellence, who will not be approached by any of us except through faith in Jesus Christ and him crucified. The unrenewed, when alarmed and excited to a high degree, if assured that they have full ability to do all that is required of them—that no radical change is necessary, may submit to God as a Being infinitely superior, and may be pronounced converts, without faith in Jesus Christ. They might be infidels before their conversion, and may be infidels still. There is, we know, a great variety of truths in the volume of revelation, which are not peculiar to Christianity.

2. However great the external reformation of an individual—however zealous he may be in his endeavors to suppress vice, and to promote the general cause of benevolence and of religion, if he do not receive Christ in all his offices, his hope can be of no value. Christianity is a system of truths, none of which are discoverable by the light of reason. They must be received on the testimony of God, and not on the ground of their apparent reasonableness to the natural man. They

must be clearly exhibited to the minds of men, or they cannot become Christians, though they may be powerfully affected, and pass from a state of deep distress to a state of peace and great joy. The human mind cannot endure for a long time a high degree of excitement. When it subsides, the quietude which is experienced is often believed to be a proof of conversion.

It is a remarkable fact that those whose conversion has been described, are of all men most opposed to the peculiar doctrines of Christianity. When Jesus said to the multitudes that followed Him, "Therefore said I unto you, that no man can come unto me, except it were given to him of my Father, many were offended. From that time many of His disciples, not of the twelve, went back and walked no more with Him." Those, who from imperfect views of Christianity, indulge a hope of salvation, and, for a time, manifest great zeal in the cause of religion, may, when the whole truth is exhibited, become its most bitter enemies. Many such facts have been known.

3. Permit me, brethren, to make the inquiry, are not many discourses delivered in which the doctrines of the cross are not made sufficiently prominent? The law ought, indeed, to be faithfully presented to the minds of men in all its extent and spirituality. They should be made to feel their obligation to be perfectly holy. For, by the law is the knowledge of sin. No one will or can come to Christ till cut off from all dependence on the law as a covenant of works. Gal. ii. 19, 20, "For I through the law," said the apostle, "am dead to the law that I might live unto God. I am crucified with Christ, nevertheless I live; yet not I, but Christ liveth in me: and the life which I now live in the flesh, I live by the faith of the

Son of God, who loved me, and gave Himself for me." The apostle was desirous that the impression made on the minds of his hearers should correspond with his own feelings and experience.

It requires great decision and moral courage at the present day to enable preachers to confine themselves to their appropriate work. They must do this, or fail of accomplishing the great object of the Christian ministry. How often has the pulpit been desecrated by unconverted, and perhaps infidel lecturers !

The recollection of the amusing anecdotes of such persons, introduced to render their performances acceptable to the multitude, renders almost powerless the messages of God delivered in the same place.

Our dependence for success must be on God. Duty is ours, events are the Lord's. All endeavors to increase the number of converts by accommodating christianity to the laws of human, unsanctified reason, is ruinous to the souls of men. There is solemnity and power in those discourses which make God prominent. It is surely unreasonable to reject doctrines clearly revealed, if they do not appear reasonable to us. We cannot by searching find out God ; we cannot know all the reasons which influence his decisions. " Thus saith the Lord," is a better reason and a better argument, and makes a deeper and more lasting inpression on the minds of men, than Thus saith the most learned philosopher or divine. The more unreservedly we trust in God, the more he will be disposed to bless us.

4. Those doctrines which are best suited to produce sound conversions, are also best suited to promote the piety of christians. It is a fact that those churches which are favored with

a ministry which give prominence to the doctrines of the cross, are most spiritual. They are not often found stupid or sleeping. They are either rejoicing in the presence of the Spirit, or mourning his departure. They can hardly hear the name of Christ crucified pronounced, without perceiving a movement of their feelings. They are the most liberal in the promotion of every enterprise, the object of which is either the spread of the Gospel in heathen lands, or the diffusion of Scripture knowledge in their own land. They are bold and decided in contending for the faith once delivered to the saints. The more intense their love of Christ, the more they love the doctrines peculiar to christianity, and the more they are grieved when they are perverted, modified, or excluded from the preached word. Nothing delights them so much as to behold the changes produced by the power of the Holy Spirit, accompanying the plain exhibitions of the doctrines of the cross.

5. It may be remarked that the fact of the death of Christ as our substitute, who stood in the room of sinners, and to which the whole volume of revelation has reference, affords the most convincing proof that all who persevere in unbelief must perish. Particular passages of Scripture which prove the doctrine of future punishment, may be perverted by learned men. But the *fact* of the death of Christ cannot be questioned. It is evident from the Scriptures that Christ did not suffer on account of any fault of his own—that he died, the just for the unjust, and that he suffered death that those who deserve death may through faith in him obtain everlasting life. The argument is conclusive. If God spared not his only begotten and dearly beloved Son, the brightness of his glory, and the express image of his person, when he stood in the room of sinners; how can any expect that he will spare them if

they refuse to accept the offers of salvation through faith in him? If it be not necessary for God to execute the penalty of his law, he surely would not have permitted his beloved Son to suffer death to effect the redemption of men.

It is too manifest to be questioned, that God is determined to execute his law, and to punish with awful severity all who persevere in impenitence and unbelief.

Can you, my brethren, meditate on the great price paid for your redemption, and not perceive your affections flow out to him, who though rich, became poor for your sakes, and who, though the only and eternally begotten Son of God, gave his life to save you? Let your thoughts be fixed on him, if you would experience a foretaste of that happiness prepared for all the redeemed. The more perfectly you understand and the more ardently you love the doctrines of the cross, the less you will be disposed to speak, to think or to hear of anything else.

If there be any present still unrenewed, let me persuade you to fix your thoughts on Jesus Christ, and him crucified. Why, think you, did he suffer death? He was holy, harmless, undefiled and separate from sinners. Do you say God is so merciful that he will not punish you, if you do not believe in his Son? But merciful as he is, when his Son took the place of sinners, and most needed some expression of his love, he hid his face from him and left him to suffer alone the penalty of his law. How can you escape if you neglect so great salvation? Christ, by his Spirit, is now near you. You need not leave your seats to find him. "And him that cometh unto me," he said, "I will in no wise cast out." Be persuaded to come to him without delay. "Behold, now is the accepted time; behold now is the day of salvation!"

The present opportunity will soon be past, and past forever.

To-morrow it may be too late. To-morrow, sinner, you may be in eternity. If not, the Holy Spirit may cease to strive with you, and may never return to you again. What more can the preacher do than point out the way of salvation, and press you to pursue it? The most essential truths of Christianity have been plainly declared, and without any modification. It remains for you cordially to receive them, if you would escape the wrath of an angry God. If you reject them you will be guilty of that suicide, where more than blood is spilt. May God, who is mighty in power and rich in grace, make his word effectual to the salvation of us all. Amen.

THE UNCTION OF THE SPIRIT.

1 JOHN II. 27.

"But the anointing which ye have received of Him abideth in you, and ye need not that any man teach you; but as the same anointing teacheth you of all things, and is truth and is no lie, and as it hath taught you, ye shall abide in Him."

THE anointing with precious ointment the priests under the former dispensation, was a visible sign of their consecration to the service of God. (Ex. xl. 15.) Their anointing was typical of the anointing or unction of the Holy Spirit under the present dispensation. Kings were anointed as well as priests. Saul and David were anointed when called of God to reign over the tribes of Israel. The anointing of priests and kings was typical of the anointing of Him who is both our great High Priest and Lord. The 6th verse of the 2d Psalm might be rendered according to the original. "Yet have anointed my king upon my holy hill of Zion." The meaning is, I have firmly established my king upon my holy hill of Zion. The Psalm is a remarkable prediction of Christ, the firm establishment of his kingdom in the world, the opposition to it of the kings and rulers of the earth, and his final triumph over all his enemies. In the 61st chapter of the prophecy of Isaiah, we find a remarkable prediction of the anointing of Jesus with the Holy Spirit. The following is the prediction. (Isa. lxi. 1, 2.) "The Spirit of the Lord is upon me, because He hath anointed me to preach the gospel to the poor; he hath sent me to heal the broken-hearted, to preach deliverance to the captives, and recovering of sight to the blind, to set at liberty them that are bound. To preach the acceptable year of the Lord." (Luke iv. 18, 19.) When in the synagogue of Nazareth, he said, "This day is this scripture fulfilled in your ears." The effect was immediately noticed by those who heard him speak. And all bear him witness, and wondered at the gracious words which proceeded out of his mouth. When he was baptized, the heaven was opened, and the Holy Ghost descended in a bodily shape like a dove upon him, and a voice came from heaven, which said, "Thou art my beloved Son, in thee I am well pleased." (Luke iii. 22.) The visible dispensation continued till the resurrection of Christ. The harmless dove was a beautiful emblem of the Holy Spirit and of the spirit of Christ.

Now, as Christ was anointed with the Holy Spirit, when he was qualified for the offices he was appointed by his Father to execute; so all, who are effectually called to be saints, are anointed with the Holy Spirit, and those who are called to minister in holy things receive a double portion of the Holy Spirit. That all called to be saints are anointed, is manifest from the text and from other passages. But ye have an unction from the Holy One, and ye know all things. 2 Cor. i. 20, 21, " Now He which stablisheth us with you in Christ, and hath anointed us is God; who also hath sealed us, and given us the earnest of the Spirit in our hearts." "Now, if any man have not the Spirit of Christ," said the Apostle Paul to the Romans, "he is none of his." (Rom. viii. 9.) Now, if every one who has been called by the Holy Spirit to be a saint, has been anointed with the same Holy Spirit with which Christ was anointed, it becomes our important inquiry, how shall we know whether we have been anointed, or whether we have the Holy Spirit dwelling in us? "Of his fulness," said John, "have we all received grace for grace." (i. 26.)

1. All Christians have been born of the Holy Spirit. "Except a man be born of water and of the Spirit, he cannot enter the kingdom of God. That which is born of the flesh is flesh, and that which is born of the Spirit is spirit." (John iii. 5, 6.)

That which is born of the Spirit is holy; and it possesses all the powers of a new creature. It is a new creature—a new man—called also the inner man. That which is born of the Spirit is united in this life with that which is born of the flesh—called the old man, and outer man. Though we are assured that they are thus united, yet we cannot fully understand and describe their union. A struggle and a warfare commence as soon as any one is born of the Spirit; the flesh lusting against the Spirit, and the Spirit against the flesh.

Now, that which is born of the Spirit is at first but a babe, whose powers are feeble; but it is immortal. As its nature is perfectly holy, it cannot sin; i. e. sin never *originates* in the new holy nature. The Apostle John, in the following passage, had reference to this new creature, this holy nature. "Whosoever is born of God doth not commit sin; for his seed remaineth in him; and he *cannot* sin, because he is born of God." (John i. 3, 9.)

The Apostle Paul had reference to his new nature, or that which was born of the Spirit, in the following passage. "For I know that in me (that is in my flesh) dwelleth no good thing: for to will is present with me; but how to perform that which is good I find not. For the good that I would, I do not; but the evil which I would not, that I do. Now, if I do that I would not, it is no more I that do it, but sin that dwelleth in me." The language of the Apostle in the passage quoted, is the language of the new man, the anointed—the Christian. The very name, Christ, signifies anointed—and the name Christian signifies anointed. The new man is a subject of the kingdom of Christ; bound to obey his laws, and to look to him for protection, and for covenant blessings.

It may also be observed, that which is born of the Spirit continually increases in strength to mortify the deeds of the body. "And we know," said the Apostle, in his epistle to the Romans, "that all things work together for good to them that love God, to them that are called according to his purpose." (viii. 28.) Grace in the heart may very justly be compared with a little leaven, which a woman took and hid in three measures of meal till the whole was leavened. That which is born of the Spirit continues to increase in power till he breaks the cords which bind him to the flesh, and he leaves the earth, to dwell forever near his Redeemer. Even the imperfections of Christians, when they review any portion of their life, lead them to humble themselves, and to make them feel their dependence on God.

2. The anointing of the Holy Spirit consists in the communication of Divine grace to the christian. The very commencement of the christian life, is the effect of the supernatural operations of the Holy Spirit. So also the anointing is supernatural. Here it may be observed, the anointing of the Holy Spirit is given to different persons in different measures. Many, whose views of the plan of redemption are clear, experience the anointing of the Spirit at the time of their conversion. The change is so great, and so exactly corresponds with the Scriptures, which they have been enabled by faithful instruction, and the enlightening and convincing operations of the

Holy Spirit, to understand, that they can hardly doubt that it is saving. By the assistance of the Holy Spirit, they have such a view of the holy character of Christ, that their affections flow out to him, and they feel that they must love him, whether saved or lost. The object of their affections appears to be in reality before their minds, and so glorious that they can think of nothing else, not even of their escape from the wrath of God, and their hope of future happiness. Those whose peace and joy arise from their deliverance from the fear of everlasting misery, or their hope of future happiness, have no good reason to believe that they have experienced a saving change.

So feeble are the powers of the new creature at first, that without the anointing of the Holy Spirit, his views would be obscure and limited, and the new exercises of his mind and heart hardly to be distinguished from the old. As soon as the Holy Spirit is withdrawn for a season, the new convert is involved in darkness—the darkness of his own mind, and he fears that he has been deceived. It is sometimes long before the christian becomes firmly established. Severe trials successfully endured, do much to confirm the christian in the faith of the Gospel. We are assured that we shall not be tempted above what we are able, if faithful, to endure. "God is faithful, who will not suffer you to be tempted above that ye are able; but will, with the temptation also make a way of escape, that ye may be able to bear it." (1 Cor. x. 18.) The darkest seasons in the experience of christians are often followed by those full of light and joy. Though the Spirit of Christ dwells in all vitally united to him, yet the anointing is granted from time to time, according to the necessities of the new man. This is discoverable even by worldly men, when christians pray, and especially when ministers pray and preach. It is manifest that they speak from the deep feelings of their heart. It is a common saying of worldly men, when they hear others pray or preach, that there is no heart in their performances. There is a solemnity which attends the prayers and the preaching of men who are spiritually minded. If not the most distinguished for the powers of their mind and their extensive learning, if they have God with them, their labors will not be in vain.

Why some appear not to be favored with the anointing of the Holy Spirit at the time of their conversion, and why they are left in darkness and doubt for a long time, we know not. It may be to prepare them by a more thorough knowledge of their own hearts for difficult labors. They may not know the day of their conversion. This must lead them to search the Scriptures and their own hearts before they dare hope they have passed from death unto life. It requires time for those who had embraced previously a false religion, to free themselves from all its principles and practices. It is hardly necessary to observe that the Holy Spirit operates with the new man, that which is born of the Spirit, and his child, to enable him to resist the old man, the body of remaining sin. And it is the Spirit that does accomplish this work. Sanctification is as much the work of the Holy Spirit as regeneration. "If ye through the Spirit," said the apostle, "do mortify the deeds of the body, ye shall live."

II. I shall now proceed to give some more particular account of the anointing of the Holy Spirit.

1. It enlightens the understanding and conscience. "Ye have an unction from the Holy One," said John, "and ye know all things." The text more fully expresses the same things.

The same Spirit by which the Scriptures were inspired, dwells in every true believer, teaching the same things he finds in the volume of revelation. The intelligent christian finds nothing in the Scriptures which relates to the way of salvation, which is not written on his own heart. He may search his heart and find the Scriptures there, so far as they relate to himself. He, therefore, may be said to know all things which it is of importance for him to know. Of course, he does not depend on the experience of another, and ought not to receive the theories and opinions of men as the foundation of his faith. Religion is a personal thing. We must understand, believe and act for ourselves. We must not believe that we are christians because others think we are, encourage us to hope we are, and persuade us to enter the church. Many have been lost, no doubt, by depending on the favorable opinion of others, and others of acknowledged piety. The intelligent christian can form a pretty correct opinion of others. Every true christian, who knows from his own experience what is essential to the character of him who has been born of the Spirit, can eaisly discover essential defects in any professed believers. When the humble and devout christian is favored with a fresh anointing from the Holy Spirit, a bright, delightful and glorious scene passes before his mind. The doctrines of christianity appear to be solemn realities, Christ appears to be the "chief among ten thousands, and altogether lovely;" the affections flow out to him, doubts are scattered, and the believer enjoys a foretaste and an earnest of heaven. His clear views of spiritual things are transforming.

2. The anointing of the Holy Spirit, which gives the christian clear views of spiritual things, enables him to declare and to defend the truths with decision and boldness. When Peter

and John had been called before the Jewish council for preaching the Gospel, and had been threatened, they still remained steadfast in the truth, fearing God rather than men. "And when they had prayed, the place was shaken where they were assembled together; and they were all filled with the Holy Ghost, and they spake the word of God with boldness." The effect of their decision and boldness was most powerful. "And the multitude of them that believed were of one heart, and of one soul: neither said any of them that aught of the things which he possessed was his own; but they had all things common. And with great power gave the apostles witness of the resurrection of the Lord Jesus: and great grace was upon them all." (Acts iv. 31–33.)

The anointing of the Holy Spirit not only enables christians to declare the truth with great decision and boldness, but makes the impression on the mind of the hearer that God is speaking to him by one of his servants. A man may be earnest, decided and bold in declaring the truth ; but, if there be not that deep feeling and solemnity in his manner, which make it manifest that he is assisted by the Holy Spirit, he will only excite opposition to the truth. Those who are not assisted by the Holy Spirit are usually timid, often withhold or modify those doctrines to which the unrenewed are most opposed. The love of human applause influences many, and men of the world love smooth things.

Discourses addressed to the imagination may draw many tears from the eyes of the speaker and of the hearer, but the heart of neither may be effected. Many theories have been devised and adopted to make it easy for men to become christians, without any radical change, or a new creation. They have always proved an injury to the church, and ruinous to the souls of very many. "If any man be a christian," said the apostle, "he is a new creature." And if any man be not a new creature, he is not a christian. A new creation is necessary to make a man a christian. Those who are favored with the anointing of the Holy Spirit, do not feel the need of any human theory to aid them. Their dependence for success is on the Spirit of God.

Where a church and its pastor are favored with the anointing of the Holy Spirit, the sanctuary is a holy place. Those who enter it feel that they are entering the presence of God, the preacher feels that his labors are connected with the honor of God, and the everlasting destiny of his hearers, and the church lift up their earnest desires for a blessing. What deep solemnity must have been upon the mind of the apostle, when he thus expressed his feelings. "For we are unto God a sweet savor of Christ in them that are saved, and in them that perish. To the one we are a savor of death unto death, and to the other the savor of life unto life; and who is sufficient for these things?"

Revivals of religion are produced by the anointing of the Holy Spirit, which extends to the whole church. What solemnity do we then discover in the house of God, in the church, in the labors of the preacher, in the congregation, now greatly increased and attentive to the word!

3. The unction of the Spirit gives vigor to all the christian graces.

"The fruit of the Spirit is love, joy, peace, long suffering, gentleness, goodness, faith, meekness, temperance; against such there is no law: and they that are Christ's have crucified the flesh with the affections and lusts." (Gal. v. 22, 24.)

Love is shed abroad in the heart by the anointing of the

Holy Spirit—love of Christ, and love of the souls of men. Intense love of any object will produce corresponding effects. It takes strong hold of him who possesses it. If we compare the love which many exhibit towards Christ and his cause, with the love they manifest for their own temporal interest we must conclude that they have not that which is essential to the christian character. How backward are many, when called upon to aid in the support of the Gospel for their families, or in sending it to the destitute, to make known to them the way of life! Can they be satisfied with their hope of future life? That love which flows from the depths of the heart, will affect the sinner, and dispose him to listen to him who seeks to do him good. The more intense our love the greater will be our exertions, and the greater liberality in the promotion of the cause of our Redeemer.

The joy, which is one of the fruits of the Spirit, is not produced so much by a belief that we have been delivered from the fear of future punishment, and have obtained a hope of heaven, as by a sense of our deliverance from the bondage of sin, and the discovery of the glory of God as it shines in the face of Jesus Christ.

On this object the christian gazes with delight and rapture. He has found him he long sought, and finds him infinitely glorious, and confesses he never before had any just conception of his excellency.

That peace, which is the fruit of the Spirit, results from reconciliation to the whole character of God, and to all the revelations he has made of himself and of his purposes. "Great peace have they that love thy law," said the Psalmist, "and nothing shall offend them. It passeth understanding." It is by faith in Jesus Christ that the controversy between the sinner and his God is terminated. Long suffering partakes of a tender and forgiving spirit. It is opposed to an irritable spirit, and is connected with patience in laboring for the happiness of our fellow-creatures. Gentleness and meekness may well be coupled together, though gentleness has reference to that kind and delicate spirit with which a christian should approach the unrenewed, and meekness to that quiet and unresisting spirit, by which he should bear rough and improper treatment. Many christians would be more successful in their attempts to do good, if they would exhibit a gentle spirit, and when opposed, would meekly bear opposition.

That goodness which is a fruit of the Spirit, is diffusive—relieving the wants of the suffering, whether the righteous or the wicked. That faith which is a fruit of the Spirit, includes faith in Christ, faith in the promises of God, and fidelity in the discharge of every duty, and in the fulfilment of every engagement.

That temperance which is the fruit of the Spirit, subjects all the passions and all the powers of the mind to the law of Christ. It is not confined merely to excess in eating and drinking, but extends to the whole man, and to the proper government of his whole life.

It is one of the evidences of true piety, and of the anointing of the Holy Ghost, that all the christian graces are exercised in perfect harmony. The operations of the Holy Spirit are not fitful and partial. They exhibit the christian character in all its just proportions, so as to correspond with the character of Christ. All the graces of the new creature increase together; otherwise his character would not be symmetrical, and could not be respected, loved and admired.

The unction of the Holy Spirit is, in a greater or less

degree, given to every christian. But it is granted to them according to their necessities, when they have made equal attainments in holiness. Those who maintain daily a holy life, enjoy constantly the presence of the Holy Spirit. As they daily commune with God, so he daily communes with them. Their conversation is in heaven, while performing the duties of the present life.

Here it may be observed, the devout christian, who has passed through many trials, and made great progress in the divine life, finds such an exact correspondence between the Scripture views of the essentials of the christian character and his own experience, that he cannot doubt that all Scripture is given by inspiration of God. An imposter might possibly describe the experience of one person for a particular day, but none but God can know and describe the essentials of every christian character, in every age, country, and at every period of life. The christian who daily meditates on the word of God for forty or fifty years, finds in the word of God an exact description of his feelings, his joys and his sorrows, his hopes and his fears. He needs no other evidence than the testimony of his own heart.

The inquiry may now be suggested to your minds, how may we obtain the anointing of the Holy Spirit?

We find that those divines and christians whose works have most of the unction of the Holy Spirit, and are most favorable to a devotional spirit in us, were called to endure severe trials, violent opposition, and many of them cruel persecution. Their trials weaned them from all attachment to the world, and led them to be much in prayer and meditation on the word of God. When they looked out upon the world, they saw the powers of the world hostile to them, the world was crucified to them, and their worldly feelings were mortified. Their place of devotion was their home, where they found a friend better than the world, who could pity them, and shed abroad his love in their hearts. Whatever tends to humble the pride of the human heart, and to mortify the deeds of the body, prepares the christian for the indwelling of the Holy Spirit. The loss of property, of health, of friends, does not humble the christian so much as the opposition and scorn of those to whom the faithful preaching of the doctrines of the cross is foolishness. It is hardly possible to describe the scorn and contempt manifested by the unitarian and infidel, when the doctrines of the cross are faithfully exhibited. The mortification of the deeds of the body, i. e. all worldly desires which are not necessary to prepare us for a discharge of our duty, and persevering prayer, prepare the heart for the indwelling and anointing of the Holy Spirit. Search your heart, and cast out everything evil, and the Holy Spirit will enter and abide there.

It was the practice of christians of former ages, when unsuccessful, to set apart days of fasting and prayer, that they might humble themselves before God, and so obtain his favor. The real christian, when unsuccessful, charges the fault to himself and not to God. By his humiliation he prepares himself for the return of the Holy Spirit, and for promised blessings. Too many, when unsuccessful, censure others, and are ready to say in their hearts, "If they were as faithful as we are, we should see a happy change." Many a time, after a day of fasting, humiliation and prayer, the Spirit has descended on the church, and on individuals who have observed such a day. "Behold, the Lord's hand is not shortened that it cannot save, nor his ear heavy that it cannot hear; but your iniquities," said the prophet, "have separated between you and your God, and your sins have hid his face from you, that he will not hear."

The Spirit of God is promised to all who ask. But those who ask, must ask in a right manner. They must feel that their own strength is but weakness, they must earnestly desire the presence of the Holy Spirit, must be untiring in the performance of their duty, must view the Holy Spirit with holy and profound reverence, must ask for things agreeable to the will of God, and with a spirit of submission to his will. A proper sense of dependence cannot be felt except by those who have exerted all their powers without success, earnestly desiring to obtain the object sought.

Let me ask the members of this church the following questions. The Spirit of God has been withholden for a long time. Have you or any of you thought yourselves faulty? have you not looked out of yourselves for the cause? One has mentioned one obstacle, and another another. Where is there one that has condemned himself? Where is there one whose tears make it manifest that he is mourning the absence of the Holy Spirit? If but a few were deeply affected, humbled on account of their sins, and could pray from the deep feelings of their heart for the Holy Spirit, we might expect to receive this great blessing. I would then say in conclusion, let every one cease to look out of himself for a reason for the continued absence of the Holy Spirit, but look into his own heart and life, for the promise is to one as well as to many. Amen.

MEDITATION.

PSALM LXIII. 5, 6.

"My soul shall be satisfied as with marrow and fatness; and my mouth shall praise thee with joyful lips: when I remember thee upon my bed, and meditate on thee in the night watches."

MEDITATION is a duty, which, I am persuaded, is less perfectly understood, and more generally neglected than any other which is equally important. Modern writers, the most pious as well as the most learned, have scarcely noticed it in their numerous publications. Who among us has ever listened to a discourse in which it was explained and enforced, or in which it was made prominent? It was a remark of Luther, one of the greatest divines and reformers that ever lived, that three things are necessary to make a good minister, and we may add a useful Christian; namely, temptation, prayer, and meditation. On the two former subjects we often hear sermons, or read essays. Every young preacher, whatever his sentiments, has a sermon on prayer, and every pastor occasionally dwells on the temptations or trials of Christians. Why, it may be asked, is the duty of meditation overlooked, which is so often mentioned, not only in the devotional parts of Scripture, but also by the most eminent saints of former ages? "Blessed is the man," said the Psalmist, "that walketh not in the counsel of the ungodly, nor standeth in the way of sinners, nor sitteth in the seat of the scornful: but his delight is in the law of the Lord; and in His law doth he meditate day and night. O how I love thy law! It is my meditation all the day." Very many passages might be selected from the Scriptures to prove that eminent saints were much accustomed to meditate on the word and works of God, and that they felt this to be a duty, on the right performance of which their advancement in holiness and true happiness very much depended. There is one passage (Ps. xxxix. 3) worthy of particular notice: "My heart was hot within me, while I was musing (or meditating) the fire burned; then spake I with my tongue." While the pious Psalmist was meditating on a subject, suggested to his mind by some event of divine providence, or by the particular circumstances of his life, the hidden fires of his soul were kindled to a flame, and from the abundance of his heart he could but speak of the things of the kingdom of God. If we go back to the 17th century, and to periods still more remote, we shall find that the most spiritual writers often brought to view the duty of meditation—that it occupied much of their time, and was thought peculiarly suited to strengthen their graces, and to give peace to their troubled minds. And will any deny that their piety was of a deeper tone than that of modern divines and Christians, and that the works of the former are much better adapted to promote a spirit of devotion than the works of the latter? Those spiritual views of divine truth, which so much delight us in the works of Baxter, Flavel, and Owen; Shaw, Charnook, How, and others, are not to be discovered in the productions of the most celebrated divines of the present century. The multitude of ephemeral publications, which only glance at subjects of the deepest interest, so occupy the minds of Christians and Christian ministers, as to leave them but little time for the study of the most valuable works, and for retirement and meditation. This is an age distinguished for enterprise and activity. Every week brings us intelligence from almost every part of the world, and the attention of Christians is directed to passing events. And it is far less difficult to observe what takes place without us than to notice carefully the operations of our own minds. What the church has gained in activity and benevolent efforts, she seems to have lost in seriousness and purity. She feels less her dependence on God, and relies more on her own wisdom and power than formerly. It may be added, those who feel it to be their duty to contend earnestly for the faith once delivered to the saints, when engaged in any controversy with learned and subtle opponents, soon become so excited, as to lose their relish for those topics which have special reference to a holy, spiritual, and heavenly life. Meetings for religious worship, and for the promotion of the objects of benevolent societies may be multiplied, till we lose all spirituality in the performance of duty. It is not the number of prayers which God regards so much, as the spirit with which they are offered. And it is not so much the amount contributed, which gives value to our offerings in the sight of God, as the disposition or motive with which we give for the promotion of any good object. How many prayers are offered which have nothing of the unction of the Spirit! And how many in their charities are uninfluenced by a regard to the glory of God!

The character of the Christian church has, during the last half century, been gradually and imperceptibly changed. What she has gained in some things, has made her overlook and forget what she has lost in other things. Indeed, she imagines that she has made as great advancement in every thing essential as she has made in activity and benevolent efforts. This is by no means the fact. It certainly is high time to call back the attention of Christians to those subjects which have been too long neglected, and which are intimately connected with their advancement in holiness.

In the following discourse I propose to explain and enforce the duty of meditation.

I. To explain the duty of meditation.

It may appear to you at first view, that this is a duty you all understand. No doubt you all have a limited and superficial view of it. There are some subjects of great practical importance, which have long been so familiar that few have ever thoroughly examined them, so as to derive from them that benefit which a perfect understanding of them might afford them. One of them, meditation, I propose now to consider.

Meditation is that act of the mind, by which all its thoughts and powers are concentrated, and fixed exclusively on some particular subject, till it produces its legitimate effects on the conscience and heart.

"To think closely and seriously on any thing," says Calmet, "is the principal and most usual acceptation of the verb to meditate." "It is," says Bennet, in his Christian Oratory, "a fixed, solemn survey or consideration of some or other subject of religion, in order to raise the affections, form pious resolutions, improve the mind, and converse with God. It is," he adds, "a fixed, solemn consideration of a subject, in which it differs from more slight and transient thinking, even upon divine matters. It is a designed, close examination of this or that argument or text, searching into the meaning, laying open the truths contained in it, making application of all unto ourselves, by way of admonition, reproof, exhortation, mixing spiritual affections therewith, as sorrow, repentance, self-indignation, love, joy, &c., endeavoring by all means to carry on some intercourse with heaven." "It is," says Baxter, "the work of all others, the most spiritual and sublime, and, therefore, not to be performed by a heart that is merely carnal and earthly. It must have all the powers of the soul, to distinguish it from the common meditations of students; for the understanding is not the whole soul, and, therefore, cannot do the whole work." Meditation not only calls into exercise all the powers of the soul, but so concentrates their force, that they act with united energy, not only in the investigation of difficult subjects, but also in the discharge of difficult duties. It is like a burning-glass, which by collecting the rays of the sun to a point, kindles combustible substances to a flame. As the rays of the sun, except when thus collected, do not produce the effect mentioned, so the operations of the mind, except when united, do not kindle to a flame the latent fires of the soul. Meditation may also be compared to the process of digestion in animal economy, without which our food can afford us no nourishment. The truths and precepts of revelation will not benefit us, unless we correctly understand them, cordially receive them, and govern ourselves according to them.

To mention some particulars.

1. When a text, or any portion of Scripture is selected for the subject of our meditation, a correct understanding of it is the first thing to be obtained. In the accomplishment of this object we must examine the connexion; ascertain, if possible, the design of the sacred penman; compare scripture with scripture, not only that one passage may explain another, but that we may obtain different views of the subject of consideration. The mere fact that the text or passage selected was penned by one who wrote as he was moved by the Holy Spirit, naturally leads us to contemplate the character and labors of the writer—the

great condescension and benevolence of God in furnishing us with the most valuable instruction—and also His rich grace in providing for us a Saviour, whose mediation is the great subject which extends through the whole volume of revelation. Here a wide field opens to view, the utmost bounds of which we can never reach.

When we understand what doctrine is taught, or what precept is contained in a text, we should next ascertain what place the doctrine occupies in the system of Christian truth, or what place the precept occupies in the system of Christian morality. Now, as all the truths peculiar to Christianity constitute one beautiful and perfectly harmonious system, we cannot dwell on any one of them without being insensibly led to admire the wisdom and benevolence of God manifested in its adoption. So, likewise, all the precepts of the gospel constitute one perfect system, according to which the Christian character must be formed. We cannot, therefore, dwell on any one of them without being led to a view of the rest. We do not properly understand a subject, unless we understand its connexion with other subjects. Many who read the Scriptures are like those travelers who pass too rapidly over a country to obtain any very particular or satisfactory views of any part of it. They can say that they have seen certain cities and villages, but what account can they give of them? Meditation removes from the word of God the veil spread over it by the indulgence of a worldly or self-righteous spirit, and enables us to discover the beauty and excellency of spiritual things. It presents to our mind a true standard, by which we may judge correctly of ourselves and of our conduct. Meditation on any scripture subject, as it is a vigorous action of the soul, seems to imply a strong desire to know the truths we ought to believe and the precepts we ought to practice. It makes us acquainted with every thing we ought to know and every thing we ought to do. Here it may be remarked, the Scriptures are always a new book to him who meditates most intensely on any portions of them. They are a treasure which can never be exhausted. Those who read the Scriptures the greatest number of times, and with the greatest care, are as much delighted with the freshness of novelty as those who have read them but a very few times.

Meditation may well be compared to a microscopic glass, by which many beauties are discovered, which without it would escape our notice. The more intense our meditation, the greater is the variety of the objects presented to our view, and the more glorious they appear.

2. Self-application is an essential branch or part of meditation. The truths we find in the word of God, when understood, we apply to our own hearts. As the work of sanctification progresses we become more and more perfectly acquainted with the character and will of God, and more and more perfectly reconciled to all the truths of his word. The new convert is reconciled to all the leading truths of God's word. But his views of the doctrines of revelation are general. As he progresses in holiness they become more particular, and the application of them is more particular. That variety of feelings which the different circumstances in which he is placed call into exercise, are tried by the truths of God's word. No man has a right to be satisfied with his hope so long as his heart is opposed to any truth plainly revealed in the word of God. That faith which is connected with the promise of salvation, is not limited, but embraces without any reserve, every truth. And that ignorance of the truth, which arises from

unsanctified feelings, or the indulgence of sinful propensities cannot be excused in the sight of God. The Jews crucified the Son of God, because they knew not what they did. Had they known, and not dared to do it, their feelings would have been the same. Their ignorance was the occasion of their acting out the feelings of their heart, which were opposed to the true character of God. Their ignorance did not excuse them in the sight of God.

A wicked man may, without any just cause, hate a good man, whose character he knows, but whom he does not know personally. They may meet without knowing each other, and the wicked man, because ignorant that he is in the presence of the good man, may, giving vent to the enmity of his heart, revile him, using the most bitter expressions. Now the fact that the wicked man did not know that he was in the presence of the good man, and too, the fact that he would have concealed his feelings had he known it, by no means excuses his conduct, or alters in the least the character of it.

In meditation, the precepts of the Gospel are applied to the feelings of our heart and to our manner of life. And the more intensely we meditate on the law of God, the more we shall be convinced that it is exceeding broad, and the more we shall think of every precept. Our knowledge of the divine law is increasing during our whole life. We are constantly looking back upon our past life and condemning actions we once thought innocent or harmless. If faithful in our meditations, we shall condemn in ourselves what the law of God condemns, and approve only what the law of God approves. The views which some have of the divine law, are so superficial that without any reproofs of conscience which trouble them, they do many things which others would not dare do. Though making pretensions to uncommon piety and zeal for God, their morality is of a very questionable character.

"To this man will I look," saith Jehovah, "to him that is poor, and of a contrite spirit, and that trembleth at my word." It is the conscientious man that trembleth at the word of God. And it is the man who is accustomed to meditate on the word of God that is conscientious. How many who make promises they never fulfil! This greatly diminishes their influence, though they may never be aware of it. Were professing Christians more strictly moral in their intercourse with worldly men, or were they more conscientious, their influence would be greatly increased. There are many worldly men, who have a high sense of justice or honesty, and veracity; and they cannot respect the professing Christian who deviates from the standard they scrupulously regard. Some, no doubt, consider their zeal in promoting objects of benevolence, or in promoting revivals, a substitute for strict morality, or at least an excuse for many errors of practice. Some of this class, though full of zeal, and apparently much engaged in religious duties, are far from being sound in doctrine, or correct in their moral conduct. Professions are of no avail if not sustained by corresponding lives. It is better not to vow than to vow and not pay. Hypocrisy is that sin which God abhors, and which men despise. Growth in grace is always manifested by increased tenderness of conscience in regard to every acknowledged duty.

II. I shall now attempt to enforce the duty of meditation.

1. We are expressly required by Jehovah himself, to meditate on his law. "This book of the law shall not depart out of thy mouth; but thou shalt meditate therein day and night, that thou mayest observe to do according to all that is written

therein: for then thou shalt make thy way prosperous, and then thou shalt have good success." (Josh i. 8.) This command is reasonable. If any business require the exercise of all the powers of our mind, it is surely that we have to transact with God, who is of purer eyes than to behold iniquity, and in whose sight the heavens are not clean. It is not sufficient to worship him with our lips, when our hearts are far from him. How few of the prayers offered to God express deep feelings of heart! And how can the heart be properly affected except by meditation on the word of God! Professing Christians may become so accustomed to perform the religious duties of every day, as to discharge them without being more affected than repeating a speech of some one of the ancients. We all know from our own experience, that our prayers become formal if we neglect only for a few days the work of self-examination, and that application of the word of God to our own hearts which results from meditation. We may be formal when we are not confined to an exact form of words, but when we feel not the power of divine truth.

It is not treating God with that reverence which he has a right to expect from us, to read the volume of revelation with no more attention than we read the works of men. The intelligence communicated is most important and interesting. It deeply concerns us for time and for eternity. What must we think of those preachers, who are so imperfectly acquainted with the Scriptures, as to be unable to repeat the texts which prove the doctrines they profess to believe! Apostasy in the church may, it is believed, be traced to neglect of the Scriptures in every instance, and to the adoption of some system of philosophy, the invention of man. Those systems of philosophy which are the offspring of the human mind, can never explain the phenomena of grace or of the operations of the Spirit. It is written, "in the wisdom of God, the world by wisdom knew not God." That system of truth which makes us acquainted with the true character of God, was never discovered by human reason; but is derived from revelation. Would any one, therefore, know the character of the true God, his law, and the way of salvation, he must search the Scriptures daily, and meditate on them day and night. This is the more important, as there is such a diversity of opinion among those who profess to believe the Scriptures to be the word of God. Such is the worth of the soul, that no one ought to be in doubt with respect to the truths which most deeply concern him.

It may be added in connexion with what has been said respecting the command of God, that those who were inspired, and who were most favored with the teachings of the Holy Spirit, were most accustomed to meditate on the word of God. The example of inspired men, speaking or writing as moved by the Holy Spirit, may be considered as a safe interpretation of the divine law. "O, how I love thy law," said the Psalmist, not finding words sufficient fully to express the feelings of his heart. He added, "It is my meditation all the day." Now it is a fact worthy of consideration, and which ought never to be forgotten, that those subjects on which Christians most delight to meditate when their minds are most spiritual, or when they are most favored with the teachings of the Holy Spirit, are best suited to promote spirituality. We know that passing by a place where we once escaped some great danger, revives the feelings experienced at that place. So meditating on subjects, or passages of Scripture, which at a former time afforded us great satisfaction and

Sermon on Psalm lxiii. 5, 6.

delight, may revive those graces which before were called into exercise.

2. That unction, which gives such beauty and interest to the prayers and all the religious duties of Christians, and especially Christian ministers, it is believed none experience who are not accustomed to meditate intensely on the word of God. It is to be lamented that so few understand how great privileges they may enjoy. Few have a proper sense of their dependence on the Spirit of God. Those who have no proper sense of their dependence on the Spirit of God, do not ask or pray for this promised blessing in a right manner, and consequently do not know from happy experience how delightful it is to be favored with His presence and assistance. They trust in their own wisdom and strength. It seems to be the opinion of many, the opinion, though not openly confessed, which actually governs them, that the Holy Spirit is needed only for the conversion of sinners. The consequence is, that their prayers and their religious performances have nothing of the unction of the Spirit, and that they know not from their own feelings, how much they might be assisted by the Holy Spirit, were they to accustom themselves to intense meditation on the divine word. Christians may be fluent in conversation and in prayer; their language may be correct, and their expressions appropriate, but if they have not the anointing of the Spirit, their very best performances will not produce any very important results. Were more time spent in retirement and meditation, and less in outward duties, no doubt much more would be accomplished. Were Christians in the true sense, to go forth in the strength of their Lord, understanding and feeling that their success depends on Him, they would not so often have occasion to complain that they have spent their labor for nought.

3. Meditation is, perhaps, more productive than the performance of any other duty of that joy which is unspeakable and full of glory, and of that peace which passeth understanding. "My soul," said the Psalmist, "shall be satisfied as with marrow and fatness, and my mouth shall praise Thee with joyful lips; when I remember Thee upon my bed, and meditate on Thee in the night watches." By meditation the soul of the Psalmist was satisfied as with marrow and fatness. This figurative language is very forcible. When he called to remembrance what he had known of the goodness of God, and the many proofs he had given of his faithfulness to one as unworthy as he felt himself to be, and when he meditated on these things he was indeed happy. His views of the excellence of the divine character were clear and greatly enlarged; his hard heart became tender, and it overflowed with gratitude and love to the best of all beings. The more perfectly he became acquainted with the character of God, and the principles of his government, the more peaceful his mind was when afflicted, or when reviled. When by meditation self becomes annihilated, or we loathe and abhor ourselves and exercise sincere repentance, then we are filled with all the fulness of God. The Spirit of God dwells with those who remember him with affection and reverence, and who delight to meditate on his word and works. Those who are favored with the presence of the Holy Spirit, experience that peace which passeth understanding, and have a foretaste of heaven.

It is intense meditation on the word of God which fits Christians and Christian ministers for the discharge of every duty, and which makes every duty a delight. It is this which gives vigor to every grace, and which is a powerful means of advancing the work of sanctification in the heart. Christians make more rapid progress in their knowledge of divine things by the inward teaching of the Holy Spirit, than by reading all the publications of the day. "The heart of the wise teacheth his mouth and addeth learning to his lips." The experience of a Christian, who for many years has been accustomed to meditate on the word of God is a safer guide to an inquirer than the most learned lectures of the ablest divine, whose knowledge is not modified and corrected by deep experience. Those who have propagated the most dangerous errors, were men who trusted more to the powers of their own mind, than to the simple word of God, and a sound Christian experience.

With respect to the selection of subjects for meditation, we must be directed by our own necessities, or the peculiar circumstances of our life. The word of God helps us to understand the events of his providence, and the course of his providence helps to understand his word. Is any one afflicted? The Scriptures contain many passages adapted to give instruction, and to afford consolation to such as have lost their property, their health, or their friends. Do any in the faithful discharge of their duty suffer reproach? The Scriptures point to prophets, apostles, and even to Christ himself, who suffered not only reproach, but death for their faithfulness. "If the world hate you," said Christ to his disciples, "ye know that it hated me before it hated you. The servant is not greater than his Lord. If they have persecuted me, they will also persecute you." Are any prosperous in their circumstances? They are taught in the Scriptures that riches take to themselves wings and fly away. Do any complain of stupidity or coldness? If Christians, indeed, meditation on the sufferings and death of Christ will dissolve the hard heart, and cause its noblest feelings to flow out to God. The success of meditation depends very much on the selection of such portions of Scripture as are suited to the state of our minds.

It may be added, that our meditations may be profitable and delightful; we must have regard to times and places chosen for the performance of the duty. These circumstances are observed by men of this world in the accomplishment of any enterprise. Seed not sown at the proper season will disappoint the expectations of the husbandman. Those who would make advances in holiness, must seek for retirement, and must improve seasons when least liable to interruption. As the work is difficult, and requires the closest attention, so it admits of no diversion. We always desire retirement when we have any difficult subject under consideration. And what business is more important than that we have to transact with God ?—that which concerns the immortal soul, and which relates to the heart, which is deceitful above all things, and desperately wicked ?

APPLICATION.

In view of the subject under consideration, I would first urge Christians to accustom themselves to meditate on the word of God, that they may perform all other duties with interest. Prayer without meditation will not express the deep feelings of the heart. And meditation without prayer does not produce its legitimate effects. When the heart is properly affected by meditation, prayer is its delight. The influence of Christians would be greatly increased, were they to devote a portion of every day, or even of every week, to intense meditation, on those passages of Scripture best suited to correct what is defective in their life, or to encourage them in the discharge of duty. How different would be the state of our churches, were the professed friends of God, instead of being satisfied with the light reading of the present day, to direct their attention to the works of men distinguished for deep piety.

Christians can hardly expect to accomplish much, unless their prayers express the deep feelings of their hearts. And they cannot experience that peace which passeth all understanding, unless their hearts are in a right state. There are many who seem neither to enjoy God nor the world. It is because they neglect, or superficially perform the duties on which their life more especially depends. Christians may, while in this world, if disposed to walk with God, and to maintain constant intercourse with him, enjoy a foretaste of heaven.

It is intense meditation on the word of God, which deepens the impressions made on the minds of sinners. To avoid being seriously alarmed, they avoid meditation on those truths best suited to operate powerfully on their minds. But when an arrow directed by the Spirit of God penetrates and wounds their heart, then the duty of meditation, though painful and distressing, they cannot neglect. Can any one who has not a good hope of heaven, dwell long on the following passage, and not be affected? "And he that believeth not the Son shall not see life; but the wrath of God abideth on him."

The sinner, though influenced by selfish motives, may do much to obtain a knowledge of God, of himself, and of his duty. And the Spirit operates with the truth. Every unrenewed man will confess that the more he meditates on the word of God, the more serious his mind is, and the more anxious he is respecting his own salvation. It is testified of the Bereans, that they searched the Scriptures daily. And it is added, "Therefore many of them believed; also of honorable women which were Greeks, and of men not a few." Few, it is believed, who meditate intensely and daily on the word of God, remain long at ease, or fail of obtaining a good hope of heaven. Let it be understood, however, that it is the Spirit of God which makes his word effectual to the salvation of those who make its essential truths the subjects of their meditation. And to Him be the praise. Amen.

TAKE MY YOKE UPON YOU.

MATTHEW XI. 29.

"Take my yoke upon you, and learn of me, for I am meek and lowly in heart; and ye shall find rest unto your souls."

A CONSCIOUSNESS of guilt always produces a fear of evil. This is the immediate consequence. As the punishment is expected from the person injured, so transgressors endeavor to conceal themselves, and to flee from those whom they have offended. The greater their apprehensions of suffering according to their demerits, the greater will be their efforts to escape from him, who has power to chastise or destroy them. Nothing is more distressing to the thoughts of a guilty person than his liability to fall into the hands of the person whom he has wronged, and who is able and disposed to demand satisfaction. And the inability of the malefactor to answer the claims of justice, renders him desperate. He hates the person he has without cause injured, and would, if possible, destroy him. These observations are applicable to all men in their natural state, who are not so perfectly stupid as to be entirely destitute of moral sensibility. They are, in a measure, likewise applicable to every thoughtful and awakened sinner who does not feel the influence of renewing grace, and whose heart is unbelieving. Returning to God, or repentance, seems to him to be giving himself up to be punished and destroyed by his justly and highly offended Sovereign. God appears to him to be a great and terrible enemy. All his purposes or efforts and intentions, however highly his mind is excited, lead him to search only for relief, or for some way by which he may escape from the hand of justice. That illumination which gives a sinner a view only of his guilt, will always produce such results. We see him anxious, but whence does it arise? and whither tend? He is not grieved and broken-hearted, because he has injured God. By no means. He is troubled, because he has exposed himself by his sins to punishment; because he is detected, and he hopes in some way to effect his deliverance from the death, which his sins deserve. At one time he tries to hide his guilt—at another to excuse it. At one time he dwells on the imperfection of human nature, and the power of temptation in the present state—thus justifying himself, and tracing his sins to God as the cause; at another time he pleads that he has done all he is able in his attempts to comply with the commands of God, when, in fact, he has made no attempt to return to his offended Sovereign, but has only labored to escape from his hand, and found himself unable. At one time he blames God and his servants because they have not given him such strong views of his situation as to be sufficient to move him to escape by his own power and virtue the wrath to come. Here it is manifest that he still trusts in himself, and refuses to give himself up without reserve to God.

The guilty person cannot endure the thought of meeting the person whom he has injured. How can he, unless extremely hardened, behold him, who cannot but look upon him with expressions of anger and scorn? God is angry with the wicked every day. "He that sitteth in the heavens shall laugh (that is at the weakness, and folly of sinners)—the Lord shall have them in derision." To be smitten is quite as tolerable as to be despised. The spirit of a man will sustain his infirmity; but a wounded spirit, who can bear ?

Now God, who is infinite in knowledge, in wisdom, and in benevolence, has devised, adopted, and published a method of salvation, exactly suited to the wants of this rebellious world. Some of its prominent features, as brought to view in the text, will be noticed in this discourse.

1. The attention of the guilty and fearful are directed in the gospel to one in human nature—one born of a woman—one, who at his advent was a little child, and one too who died on the cross, the just for the unjust. Here is an object which we can contemplate, and of which we can have some idea, and on which our thoughts, accustomed to wander in darkness for a refuge, may rest. All our meditations on the attributes of Jehovah, which are discoverable by the light of nature, or of reason, leave us in total darkness with respect to our salvation. But Christ is God manifest in flesh. He is the brightness of his Father's glory, and the express image of his person.

This is an object we need not fear to behold or to approach. We can look at the holy child Jesus, because we discover in his eye pity and forgiveness, " no terrors clothe *his* brow."

It is impossible to persuade an impenitent sinner, conscious of his guilt, and terrified with apprehensions of the wrath of his offended Sovereign, to return to God out of Christ, or to return to God as revealed by the light of nature. But those who are farthest from God may be encouraged to look to Jesus, and to come to him. One object of the gospel is to make the impression on the mind of every one that hears it, that God can be just, and the justifier of him that believeth in Jesus. But it is exceedingly difficult to persuade sinners that it is safe for them to make a full confession of their sins, and to submit without reserve to Christ. They are afraid that in some way they shall fail of obtaining forgiveness. Men are not willing to bear witness against themselves, when their own testimony is to be the chief ground of their condemnation. The little child that has done wrong conceals his guilt as long as possible —endeavors to excuse it, and to hide himself from his offended parents. But the fair prospect of pardon, and of being restored to favor, may induce him to venture from his secret place, and to confess the whole truth.

It is unquestionably the fact that those now in this house who are at the greatest distance from God, and from salvation, are kept in their present state by a groundless fear of returning to God. Though they may deny or excuse their guilt; find fault with the law of God, and the doctrines of revelation; yet they cannot extinguish the light of their conscience. They feel that all is not right. In their sober moments they are unhappy. Is it not so? You are ashamed and afraid to return to God! You are unbelieving. You cannot believe that God is disposed to forgive you, or that He will behold you without strong expressions of indignation. Your secret thought is, though perhaps you are not sensible of it, should you return to God, He would frown upon you, reproach you, express contempt of you, and thrust you from his presence. It is timidity—unreasonable timidity—the timidity of guilt, which keeps many from God. The gospel is designed to remove this—to convince the sinner that with God there is forgiveness, that He may be feared. It directs your attention to the Lamb of God that taketh away the sin of the world.

2. Hear now his affectionate address to every one in this house, who is still impenitent, or who is without any good

hope of salvation. "Take my yoke upon you," he says, "and learn of me."

The meaning of the first of these clauses is easily ascertained. Though it may be impossible to obtain justification by the deeds of the law; though the sinner may despair of discharging the debt he owes to God, yet there is a way in which he may obtain justification, and in which he may be restored to the friendship of his offended Sovereign. Make no attempt, is the direction of Christ, to the anxious sinner, to work out a righteousness of your own. This is impossible. But receive my gospel—join yourself to me—trust in me—follow me—submit to my authority. I have magnified the Divine law, and made it honorable. I am the *end* of the law for righteousness to every one that believeth. All the difficult parts of the work, to which you are called, I have finished. What remains is easy and light to every one, who is disposed to do any thing for God. Nothing is required, which the person, who has any right feelings would be willing to neglect. A life of faith is a life of peace and joy. But the way of transgressors is hard.

The Christian finds nothing unreasonable in any of the requirements of the gospel. He would by no means alter those precepts which most condemn his practice. A very short experience convinces him that his Lord is ever ready to impart grace as it is needed. All, without one exception, who have received the gospel, are ready to testify that its commands are not grievous.

2. The second clause of the direction of Christ, *Learn of me*, undoubtedly has this meaning. Look to me for light—for knowledge—for wisdom in the performance of duty. Look to me for all the instruction you need, and imitate my holy

example. Willingness to be led and to be taught by Christ, are evidences of true piety. Those who have an obedient spirit are ready to keep the commands of their Lord. They always submit their will to his commands, feeling that he has a perfect right to their service. Putting no trust in their own wisdom and knowledge, they reverence the instructions of Christ, as of infinite value.

3. I shall now proceed to consider the arguments by which Christ would persuade every sinner to come to him. These are exactly suited to meet his case, and to give us a most interesting view of the character of our divine Lord.

1. Such is the natural disposition of mankind, if we except those who have been renewed, that when one has been injured, he always is offended, and seeks satisfaction. This observation is applicable to societies and nations, as well as to individuals. The guilty consequently look for punishment, if detected, and if the person injured have power to inflict it. The injured person looks with scorn on the person who has wronged him. The guilty expect rough treatment from those whom they have offended. They seem to have a consciousness of inferiority when conscious of guilt.

To such as have been accustomed to receive rough treatment from those they have injured, and who are afraid to return to God, because they have offended Him, Christ presents this motive, for *I am meek and lowly,* i. e., mild, gentle, pitiful, and forgiving.

Fear not, then, anxious sinner, to come to Christ, for he is meek. Behold him, there is nothing revengeful in his spirit; when reviled he reviled not again; when on the cross, he offered this prayer, "Father, forgive them, for they know not what they do." See him weeping over Jerusalem, the abode of his most bitter enemies; hear his lamentation, "O Jerusalem, Jerusalem, thou that killest the prophets, and stonest them, which are sent unto thee, how often would I have gathered thy children together, even as a hen gathereth her chickens under her wings, and ye would not!"

"He was oppressed, and he was afflicted, yet he opened not his mouth; he is brought as a lamb to the slaughter, and as a sheep before her shearers is dumb, so he openeth not his mouth." "He came not into the world to condemn the world, but that the world through him might be saved." He is lowly as well as meek. This spirit of superiority and pride, which the guilty are accustomed to discover in those whom they have injured, is not exhibited by Christ even to the chief of sinners, who are troubled on account of their transgressions.

How can we but admire the disposition and spirit manifested by our divine Lord towards thoughtful and anxious sinners, even the most guilty! "Be not afraid to come unto me, and take my yoke upon you," he says to those who are most deserving of the wrath of God. Come unto me, for I am meek and lowly in heart, altogether unlike your fellow-creatures, whom you have offended. You have reason to be afraid of men, whom you have injured; but you need not hesitate to return to God, whose laws you have broken. The argument, for I am meek and lowly, removes one class of obstacles to the repentance of sinners—all those objections and excuses which arise from a comparison of Christ with men, who are revengeful in their spirit, and disposed to censure without mercy the faulty. Such is the love, the intense love of Christ to perishing sinners, that he goes to those farthest from him, i. e., farthest from him by their sins, and with meekness and humility, bids them return to him without fear of reproach, censure, or scorn. Here, let it be understood, the timidity of the sinner is in proportion to his distance from God. This is true with respect to all who begin to be anxious.

The first thought of returning to God is accompanied with fear. The distance between the sinner and God is fearful; the work to be performed appears to be great—too great to be accomplished. His feelings are not in some respects unlike the feelings of the man who has enlisted as a soldier, when about for the first time to enter the field of battle; or the feelings of the man who is about to cross the ocean for the first time. The wise and prudent commander always endeavors to quiet their fears by his kind and affectionate deportment. How ought we to admire the wisdom of Christ exhibited in the argument, for I am meek and lowly! used to persuade sinners—even the chief—to return to God!

2. The second argument offered, seems to be of sufficient weight to decide a doubting mind.

"And ye *shall* find rest to your souls," he says to the anxious sinner. This is assurance. There is no doubt intimated. It is not high probability that is to persuade. This is all the officer can offer to the timid soldier, that he probably will escape death, and be victorious; this is all that can be said to the trembling seaman, when the broad ocean is before him, and the land disappears.

No one can excuse his hesitation with the plea, should I repent and come to Christ, it is doubtful whether I should find rest to my soul. It is the secret thought of some, there is no mercy for them. They believe that they are willing to return to God, but persuade themselves that he is not willing to pardon them. They believe that they are desirous of enjoying religion, but cannot obtain it. It is true there are many who are desirous of being delivered from the fear of future misery, and of obtaining the hope of future happiness. Such desires are common to all men—to the most immoral; to infidels and atheists as well as to real Christians. What virtue, it may be asked, can there be in such desires, when they are closely connected with a determination to remain in sin, in unbelief, and impenitence? Such inquiries as the following may now be proposed to those who believe they desire religion, and who believe that there is something good in their feelings. Are you grieved on account of the injury you have done to God—to his beloved Son, and to your fellow-creatures? Are you troubled at all on account of your transgressions, your numerous transgressions of the Divine law—your neglect—your long neglect of the gospel of Christ? Are you desirous of being restored to the service of God, that you may render to him his due? If the rights and claims of God, and of His Son, and the injuries you have done to them are overlooked, or are considered of less importance than your own happiness, then there can be nothing good in your anxiety, and no commencement in it of a return to your offended Sovereign. The way to life is straight and short. You have not far to travel, if you only choose the right way. But you may travel for years in the paths of error—self being the point from which you start, and to which you aim; and you may never reach heaven.

If grieved and broken-hearted on account of the injury you have done to God, and to His Son, I am authorized to say that you shall find rest to your souls. If Christ appears precious to you as one who saves from sin, and if he appears so lovely that your heart is drawn toward him, then be assured you are his. If in your prayers, your chief desires are that the kingdom of God may come, then may you conclude that they are heard. Become one with Christ in spirit, in purpose, and in interest, and you may hope to be joint heirs with him to an inheritance incorruptible, undefiled, and that fadeth not away.

The rest which Christ gives is not merely relief from distress, arising from deliverance from the fear of future punishment, and from the hope of future happiness. This, it is apprehended, is all the relief many experience. This is ruinous. When the mind of any one has been in a high degree of excitement, and it is quieted with a false hope, the case of that individual is almost desperate. This false hope becomes so deeply rooted as to remain usually till death. The rest which Christ gives is deliverance from the tyranny and the slavery of sin. It is a rest which is connected with delight and activity in the service of God, and which is connected with the hope of perfect holiness as well as happiness.

APPLICATION.

1. There are some in this house who have a hope that they have taken Christ's yoke upon them, and that they have experienced that rest which he gives to all who come to him. Does Christ now appear to you meek and lowly? amiable in his whole character, and altogether excellent? If really his disciples, you are daily coming to him, and learning of him. If his disciples, he is revealed to you by his Spirit. And the view which you have of him is transforming. To be a Christian, and not to be like your Lord is impossible. If you have tasted and seen that he is good, you can never be satisfied to be separated from him. The Christian is either rejoicing in the pres-

ence of Christ, or mourning his absence. The light which is within him can never be extinguished; the life commenced in his soul can never be destroyed.

It is a view of Christ which produces that sweetness of temper which we cannot but admire in the real convert. This is the pattern to which you must look, and to which you must look constantly. However great the change experienced by any one, if not conformed to this model, it can be of no avail.

2. There may be some in this house who are far from God, and who, though unwilling to acknowledge it, are conscious that vast mountains rise between them and their offended Sovereign. Some are without hope, who are far advanced in life. Others have been thoughtless—perhaps immoral, and perhaps have made light of religion. If you contemplate the attributes of God, and overlook Christ, the work you are required to perform will appear to be of such magnitude that you will never attempt it. Despair will settle on your mind, and this will prevent all exertions. But if you fasten your thoughts on Christ your work will appear less difficult.

The journey to be performed will appear to be short, and God will appear to be near; every valley will appear to be exalted, and every mountain and hill will appear to be made low; the crooked ways will appear to be made straight, and the rough places plain.

Look unto Jesus. What is there terrific in his countenance? Behold him! He is meek and lowly in heart. Look at him! the tear in his eye is the tear of pity; the sorrow in his countenance is occasioned by his deep feelings of compassion for sinners. Behold him dying on the cross! However formidable he may have appeared to you as an enemy, justly offended, you cannot be afraid to approach him, when you see him dying, and when you find too, that you have prevailed against him. Here you may have a view of your guilt; here you may discover what you have done, and how you must be saved, if saved at all.

3. There are some in the midst of life, and devoted to the world who, through the pride of their heart, will not seek after God, and who are far from him. If this would procure your salvation, you would not hesitate to give large sums of money for a good hope of heaven; you would not refuse to perform a long pilgrimage, you would even go to the stake. But to bow your heart to one who was the son of a carpenter—who was a man of sorrows, and acquainted with grief—who had not where to lay his head—who possessed neither the treasures of the world, nor obtained its honors—whose kingdom is spiritual, here is the difficulty. This seems to be too much. And it is still a greater sacrifice to kneel before him, and to confess that you deserve death—to look to him, and to depend on him alone for pardon.

But consider that he is meek and lowly in heart. Consider too, that you must bow or perish. There is no other alternative. For there is no other name given under heaven among men, whereby we must be saved. You now have your choice. "He that covereth his sins shall not prosper; but he that confesseth and forsaketh them shall find mercy." "Verily, I say unto you, Whosoever shall not receive the kingdom of God as a little child, he shall not enter therein." (Mark x. 15.)

You cannot go from this house, sinner, without receiving, or once more rejecting the offer of mercy. Can you again turn your back upon him who has all this day been weeping over you? Can you longer resist the Holy Spirit that has been striving with you, and laboring to effect your salvation? My Spirit, saith Jehovah, shall not always strive with man. Be persuaded to seek the Lord now, while he may be found, and to call upon him now he is near.

HEAVEN.

JOHN XVII. 24.

"Father, I will that they also whom thou hast given me, be with me where I am; that they may behold my glory, which thou hast given me: for thou lovedst me before the foundation of the world."

AFTER Jesus had for the last time partaken of the Passover with his disciples, having previously said to them that he should soon leave them, and also leave the world, and perceiving how deeply this information affected them, he addressed them in the most affectionate manner, to prepare them for the trials through which he knew they would be called to pass.

When he had finished his address, and probably before he left the guest chamber, he offered that fervent prayer recorded in the chapter from which the text has been taken.

Though about to be separated from his beloved disciples, who had been a long time with him, it was his desire and prayer that they might all meet in heaven, and all dwell together there forever. Their labors and trials, though severe, he knew would be of short duration, and not worthy of a sigh or a tear, when they had a bright view of their inheritance beyond the grave.

Jesus prayed not only for his disciples, who had been his companions during his ministry, but for all true believers, and for all who should afterward, in any part of the world, believe on him. His prayer we are sure will be answered. None who trust in him will be lost.

Much as Jesus loved his disciples, and much as they loved him, he did not pray that they might leave the world with him, and then obtain possession of the inheritance he had purchased for them. He had important work for them to do, which he knew would expose them to violent opposition and cruel persecution. He knew that some would suffer a martyr's death. Their love of him who gave his life to redeem them, made them anxious to do what they could to express their gratitude to him, and to extend his kingdom in the world. They were willing to suffer, and to expose their lives in circumstances which enabled them to give decided proofs of their love of their Master, and their firm belief of the truths of his Gospel. They needed trials to humble them, and to keep them near to God. And they needed trials to prepare them, and to make them willing to leave the world.

After his resurrection, when Jesus had showed himself alive to his disciples by many infallible proofs, being seen of them forty days, and speaking of the things pertaining to the kingdom of God, "while they beheld, he was taken up, and a cloud received him out of their sight. And while they looked steadfastly toward heaven, as he went up, behold, two men stood by them in white apparel, which also said, Ye men of Galilee, why stand ye gazing up into heaven? The same Jesus which is taken up from you into heaven, shall so come in like manner as ye have seen him go into heaven." "Behold," said the apostle John, "he cometh with clouds, and every eye shall see him, and they also which pierced him, and all the kindreds of the earth shall wail because of him." (Rev. i. 7.)

Who can have any adequate conception of the triumphal entrance of Jesus into heaven, after he had successfully performed the part assigned him on the earth, in the work of redemption ?—a work far more difficult, more important and more glorious than the work of creation. A great company of holy angels attended him, when he came down from heaven, and were ready to bid him welcome on his return. His garments of humiliation were thrown off, and he appeared in his robe of glory. All the hosts of heaven rejoiced and shouted his praise, when he again was in the midst of them, and when his Father bid him welcome, and gave him a seat at his right hand.

The following passage is descriptive of the praise and worship he received after he entered heaven, whether at the very time of his arrival or afterward the Scriptures do not inform us, nor is this material.

"And I beheld," said John, "and I heard the voice of many angels, round about the throne, and the beasts (or living creatures) and the elders: and the number of them was ten thousand times ten thousand, and thousands of thousands, saying with a loud voice, Worthy is the Lamb that was slain to receive power, and riches, and wisdom, and strength, and honor, and glory, and blessing. And every creature which is in heaven, and on the earth, and under the earth, and such as are in the sea, and all that are in them heard I saying, Blessing, and glory, and honor, and power, be unto him that sitteth upon the throne, and unto the Lamb forever and ever. And the four living creatures said, Amen, and the four and twenty elders fell down and worshiped him that liveth forever and ever."

As heaven is the place to which our Redeemer and Lord has gone, where he now is, and which will be the final home of all true believers, you, my brethren, may desire to know all that may be known of your future home, your companions, your employments and your enjoyments.

I. *The location of heaven.* With respect to the location of heaven, we can only say, heaven is where Christ is. It is above and beyond the place where we now dwell. Christ came down from heaven, and ascended up to heaven. It is where there are no terrific storms, no chilling blasts of winter, no scorching heat of summer, no pains, no diseases, no quarrels, no wars, no calamities of any kind, no death.

Now as the earth daily revolves on its axis, and yearly round the sun, when we look toward heaven we look above the earth. When Jesus ascended he was seen to go up in a cloud from the earth. But the place in the heavens which is high above us at noon, is far below us at midnight, and the latter place may be at a vast distance from the former. Great is the velocity with which the earth moves in its orbit round the sun. Wherever we are on the earth's surface, whether in America or Africa, Europe or Asia, we are equally near to heaven, and equally near to our Saviour. Though we see him not, he sees us every moment, by night and by day, knows everything we do, everything we say, and all our thoughts. In every part of the world, where two or three are met together in his name, there he is in the midst of them—only a thin curtain conceals him from them. His people, when met for prayer, often have proof of his presence by his Spirit.

The law of attraction, which draws the planets toward the sun in the solar system, and all bodies on and near the earth's surface towards its centre, is not felt by the souls of men when separated from their material bodies. The solar system, with its law of attraction, may in some particulars afford an illustration of things in the invisible and spiritual world. In the invisible and spiritual world Christ is the Glorious Sun—the centre to which all holy beings are attracted. He is the light of heaven, the invisible God manifest in human nature. Holy angels delight to behold him, and to dwell on the great work he has accomplished for the *redemption* of men. When the world was *created*, "the morning stars sang together, and all the sons of God shouted for joy." (Job xxxvii. 7.) They saw with wonder and delight, displayed in the work of creation, the power, the wisdom, and the goodness of God. Men most distinguished for the power of their minds, who have devoted their whole lives to the study of the laws of the visible world, are forced to confess that they have but just entered the threshold, so much remains to be known. The greater the attainments made in the study of any of the works of God, the less they appear when compared with what might be obtained, if life should be sufficiently prolonged. The work of redemption will never be fully understood in the future world. Wonder will perpetually succeed wonder without end. The mystery of the Trinity, the three persons equally interested in the work of redemption, saints and angels will never cease to contemplate with the most exalted thoughts of God. The work of redemption gives us more enlarged and adoring views of the character of God than his work of creation.

In heaven the *law* of *attraction* is the *law of love*, by which all the redeemed will be drawn toward their Lord, and will be kept from ever departing from him. His love will be mutual between him and all his people. His love is infinitely powerful, and shed abroad in their hearts, will enable them to love him with all their powers. The stronger their love of their Redeemer, the greater will be their happiness. Of the multitude of the redeemed, whose home is heaven, no two will probably be equally near to their Lord, because there will be some difference in the strength of their love. Some have done more and suffered more in the service of their Lord and Master. When John in vision saw some arrayed in white robes, and was desirous of knowing who they were, one of the elders said to him, "These are they which came out of great tribulation, and have washed their robes and made them white in the blood of the Lamb. Therefore are they before the throne of God, and serve him day and night in his temple, and he that sitteth on the throne shall dwell among them."

As soon as the spirit of the Christian leaves his body, and is free from the influence of that law which keeps him on the earth, the attraction of the law of love draws him toward heaven, the home of his Saviour. On rapid wing he is borne to the arms of him who gave his life to purchase his redemption.

Christ appears to occupy a central place, in the midst of the throne, and of the four living creatures, and in the midst of the elders, and to be surrounded by a great multitude, who never cease to adore and worship him.

He receives equal honor with his Father. We are required to honor him as we honor the Father. All the angels are commanded to worship him. "All things," he said, when on earth, "are delivered unto me of my Father; and no man knoweth the Son but the Father, neither knoweth any man the Father save the Son, and he to whomsoever the Son will reveal him." (Matt. xi. 27.) An infinite Spirit cannot be seen. By his works and his revelations we may obtain a knowledge of his attributes, and his character, his purposes, and the principles of his government. Christ is himself the most perfect revelation God has given of his character and purposes. He is declared to be the brightness of his Father's glory, and the express image of his person. "It hath pleased his Father that in him should all fullness dwell." (Col. i. 19.) When on earth but few rays of his Divinity appeared; but in heaven he appears to be all glorious.

The description of the New Jerusalem, which we find in the 21st chapter of the book of Revelations, is doubtless figurative, designed to convince us that the place where the redeemed will forever dwell with their adored Lord, is the most splendid and delightful in the universe. It will be far more beautiful and magnificent than any city that ever has been or can be, should all the most precious stones ever found be collected, and used in building it. The high walls denote the security of those who dwell in the city. As the redeemed will dwell together as social beings, so they are represented as dwelling together in a city of sufficient extent to include them. "And I saw," said John, "no temple therein, for the Lord God Almighty and the Lamb are the temple of it. And the city had no need of the sun nor of the moon to shine in it, for the glory of God did lighten it, and the Lamb is the light thereof."

"Eye hath not seen, nor ear heard, neither have entered into the heart of man, the things which God hath prepared for them that love him." Our loftiest conceptions of the glory of heaven must fall far below the reality. How great must be the change experienced by the christian, when he leaves the world and enters heaven!

II. Another inquiry naturally suggested to the mind when meditating on the Scripture account of heaven, is the following: What may be known of the society which the redeemed will enjoy in that holy place?

The person seen above and more glorious than all others, will be their beloved and adored Redeemer and Lord. He will appear as he appeared to Peter and James and John, when transfigured, only far more glorious. These disciples were then terrified and overpowered. Their bodies were frail, and they were not perfectly sanctified. They fell upon their faces and were sore afraid, when they had but an imperfect view of the glory in which Christ appears in heaven. His face then shone as the sun, and his raiment was so white and glistening that no fuller on earth could whiten it. When a cloud overshadowed them, there came a voice out of the cloud, saying, "This is my beloved Son in whom I am well pleased." After the resurrection of their bodies the redeemed will be like their Lord.

"Beloved," said the apostle John, "now are we the sons of God, and it doth not yet appear what we shall be; but we know that when he shall appear, we shall be like him; for we shall see him as he is." (1 John iii. 2.)

In the humiliation of Christ, the unbelieving Jews, blinded by the god of this world, saw no beauty in him that they should desire him. Their hearts were opposed to his holy character. When giving them the strongest proofs of his love of them—giving his life to save them from everlasting death, they reviled him, treated him with contempt, and rejoiced in his sufferings.

Intense meditation on the glory, the works and the doctrine of Christ, while in our present state, has a transforming influence on our character, strengthens our faith, increases our love, and fills us with joy unspeakable and full of glory. Those whose views are most spiritual, occasionally obtain glimpses of the glory of Christ, and for a season have a foretaste of the joys of heaven.

"We are," said the apostle to the Corinthians, "with open face, beholding as in a glass the glory of the Lord, are changed into the same image from glory to glory, even as by the Spirit of the Lord." (2 Cor. iii. 18.)

Christ will appear in heaven in the midst of the redeemed, constantly revealing himself more and more perfectly to them; and they will become more and more like him. When present in his church on earth by his Spirit, his people enjoy refreshing seasons, all their graces are invigorated, and their hope of future happiness and glory is bright. Though he will appear in heaven in the glory of his Father, having accomplished the work assigned him in the plan of redemption, and having triumphed over all the powers of darkness, yet he will appear so condescending and lovely, that the redeemed will approach him with as much freedom as that with which his disciples approached him when he was with them in the world. It seemed to be the belief of the apostle Paul, that as soon as he left the body he should be with Christ. "For," he said, "I am in a strait betwixt two, having a desire to depart and to be with Christ, which is far better. We are confident and willing, he said, to be absent from the body, and to be present with the Lord."

The most perfect freedom of intercourse will be enjoyed by the great company of the redeemed. Though some will have made greater attainments than others, and shine brighter than others, yet the more distinguished any are for holiness, the more they will be distinguished for humility. Pride will be unknown in heaven. All will feel that they are indebted to the distinguishing grace of God for the places they occupy—that God might have been just in their final condemnation and punishment. The recollection of their state by nature, and their continued opposition to the doctrines of grace, and resistance of the Holy Spirit, till the power that created them anew in Christ Jesus will keep them humbled. As they will enjoy the society of the patriarchs, the prophets, the apostles, the martyrs, those who were in the world, rich and poor, high and low, who died young, and who lived to old age, they will be able to learn of them the wonderful and various operations of the Holy Spirit.

Who can read the history of the patriarchs without a desire to see and converse with them?—the Psalms, without a desire to unite with David in the praise of God?—the *books of the Prophets*, without a desire to see the authors?—*the epistles*, without a desire to converse with the apostles?—the book of Revelation, without a desire that John would explain the dark passages we do not now understand? The history of every saint will have some peculiarities sufficient to fill a volume. The histories of all the redeemed, if written, would fill heaven with books. There will be variety in the experience of the redeemed in heaven, corresponding with their attainments in this world.

If now we consider the thousands, and tens of thousands, and thousands of thousands now in heaven, and the vast multitude to be added to them, the variety in their experience of the grace of God, it must be manifest that we never can know all that may be known of the wonders of redeeming love.

Holy angels who are ministering spirits to the church on earth, will be the companions of the redeemed in heaven. They will never cease to feel an interest in those whom they assisted in their pilgrimage in the world. We know very little of the ministry of angels under the present dispensation, as they have not been visible, if we except a short period after its commencement. We cannot doubt that their influence is felt, that holy angels minister to the righteous, and evil spirits strengthen the evil propensities of the wicked. Holy angels will be willing to communicate to the redeemed all they know of the part they performed in their salvation.

When all the vast multitude in heaven unite with all their hearts in the worship of God, to whom holy angels as well as the redeemed are indebted for his distinguishing goodness, how powerfully must every one be affected! More powerful impressions we know, are made in a great assembly than in a social circle, where few are met together.

III. *The employments of the redeemed in heaven.*

Already we have noticed some of the employments of the redeemed.

The views which some have of the employments of saints in heaven appear to me to be very imperfect, and to be derived from their experience of the most agreeable worldly employments. Now, the employments of this world which are most agreeable, and which men most desire, are freest from labor, and from all vigorous exertion of mental or physical power. Men in the pursuit of wealth look forward to the time when they shall have no occasion to labor, and shall be able to rest in the quiet enjoyment of their possessions. The day laborer looks forward to the hour when his work will be done, and he shall enjoy comfortable repose. So the traveller looks forward with satisfaction to the rest he expects to enjoy when his journey is finished. But the christian who has made the greatest progress in holiness, thinks least of what he has done, and hopes when free from his body that he shall be able to serve God more faithfully. This desire to be free from the body is not that he may rest, but that he may be more active than ever in doing the will of God.

It is true, christians when they die, rest from their worldly labors. The Scriptures, when they notice the rest of the people of God, have reference to the termination of the labors performed for their temporal support. Now, if the chief object pursued by the christian be perpetual and uninterrupted happiness, the hope of enjoying which sustains him in all his trials, and moves him to act, he is selfish, he may be as selfish in seeking future as present happiness.* The christian does not desire heaven merely or chiefly that he may be more happy, but that he may be free from sin, and may more perfectly worship God. When the exercises of his mind are most powerful, he finds that he cannot do the good he would.

"For the good that I would," said the apostle, "I do not; but the evil which I would not, that I do." Now the apostle had in view more powerful exercises of his whole soul in the worship of God, when free from the remains of sin. His desire was that he might be free from all sin, and all hindrances, that he might worship God with the most vigorous exercise of all his powers. The trials the Christian experiences in this life are designed to promote the work of sanctification in his heart—to enable him to overcome and subdue his worldly inclinations—to draw him nearer to God, and thus to qualify him to worship Him more acceptably. Why should Christians desire to be free from the most salutary discipline ordered and directed by their heavenly Father? "The Lord gave and the Lord hath taken away," said Job, "and blessed be the name of the Lord." The redeemed in heaven may have some

---

* "Nor indeed can there be a vainer or more absurd design and expectation, than to aim immediately at delights and joys without ever looking after that transforming, purifying, quickening communication from God, in which he is to be enjoyed, which is apparently the most dangerous and prejudicial mistake of many persons of much pretence to religion, that dream and boast of nothing else than raptures and transports, having never yet known or felt what the work of regeneration or the new creature means."—*Howe, vol.* 1, *p.* 324.

"They desire happiness without labor."—*A divine of* 17*th century.*

employment of which we now have no knowledge. They may with holy angels be ministering spirits to the church till the end of the world.

Is there not reason to believe that the redeemed in heaven will pray as well as praise till the work of redemption is completed? It was the observation of an old and orthodox divine not long since, that this was his opinion, and that its abuse was the reason it was not expressed. If any man have not the Spirit of Christ, said the apostle, he is none of his. Those who are most eminent for piety have most of the spirit of Christ. Can we suppose that when they leave the world, the spirit of Christ will depart from them? Now the spirit of Christ is a spirit of intercession. Wherefore, said the apostle, treating of the priesthood of Christ, he is able also to save them to the uttermost, that come unto God by him, seeing he ever liveth to make intercession for them. The spirit of intercession is a spirit of prayer. Now, believers are vitally united to Christ, as the members of the body to the head, or as the branch to the vine. They are one with him. His Spirit dwells in them. When he intercedes for his church on earth, and for all given to him by his Father, may we not conclude that all the redeemed in heaven will be united with him by his Spirit in the intercession? Can the redeemed when they enter heaven forget those they left behind? Can parents forget their children—children their parents—husbands their wives, or wives their husbands—brothers their sisters, or sisters their brothers? Can faithful pastors forget those for whose salvation they labored and prayed; some of whom were converted by their ministry?

The following passages we find in the revelations of things in heaven made to the apostle John. "And another angel came and stood before the altar, having a golden censer; and there was given him much incense that he should offer it with the prayers of all saints upon the golden altar, which was before the throne, and the smoke of the incense, which came with the prayers of the saints, ascended up before God out of the angels hand." (Rev. viii. 4.) "And when he had opened the fifth seal, I saw under the altar the souls of them that were slain for the Word of God, and for the testimony which they held: and they cried with a loud voice, How long, O Lord, holy and true, dost thou not judge and avenge our blood on them that dwell on the earth? And white robes were given unto every one of them, and it was said unto them, that they should rest yet for a little season, until their fellow-servants also, and their brethren, that should be killed as they were, should be fulfilled." (Rev. vi. 9, 10, 11.) In this last passage there is a prayer offered with earnestness by those who had been slain, and whose souls were in heaven. (See Rev. xix. 10.)

When pious friends are removed from us by death, it must afford much consolation to those who survive, if they may indulge the hope that their departed friends still feel interested in their welfare, and are permitted to pray for them. It cannot be doubted that the saints in heaven feel interested in the cause of their Redeemer, and that they greatly desire that the number of His disciples in this world may be increased. If there is joy in heaven in the presence of the angels over one sinner that repenteth, then we must conclude that events on earth are known in heaven. "All the powers of the saints in heaven will be exercised to the highest degree. Though they rest from their labors on the earth, yet we are assured that in the worship of God, they rest not day and night." (Rev. iv. 8.)

There is then a sense in which there is no rest in heaven—no cessation of the most powerful exercises of the soul. The Christian in this life, when a subject of the powerful operations of the Holy Spirit, worships God with all his heart, and the perfect freedom he experiences from all worldly influences is an earnest and foretaste of that rest he will enjoy in heaven. Christ, we are assured, ever liveth to make intercession for his church on earth. (Heb. vii. 25.) How unhappy must those be, if admitted into heaven, to whom it is a weariness to go to the house of God, and who are weary in His service when there—impatient to have the service ended! They seem not to be aware, if they enter heaven, they must there serve God night and day. It is only the unrenewed and worldly minded who find the service of God tedious. As churches depart from God, their services are shortened, and they are satisfied with superficial and modified views of the truth. They desire something amusing. (Rev. xix. 10.)

IV. *The enjoyments of the redeemed in Heaven.* They will be highly honored, and distinguished from the rest of the human race.

They will be near to their adored Lord, and will constantly behold him. When in this world they obtain but a glimpse of His excellence; they are filled with joy unspeakable and full of glory. They will, while praising Him, receive from His inexhaustible fullness constant communications of good, which will make them unspeakably happy. They will experience perfect satisfaction. As the tree of life, which John saw bears twelve manner of fruits, so we may suppose that there will be some variety in the enjoyments as well as employments of the redeemed, and that every holy desire will be gratified. The more active, the more happy they will be, Christ will constantly and forever be revealing himself to all the redeemed. This increase of knowledge will be a constant source of happiness. We can never know all that may be known of God. Every new revelation will open a new field of contemplation. The inheritance of believers will be as large as their desires, and as lasting as their existence. "Blessed be the God and Father of our Lord Jesus Christ," said the apostle Peter, "who according to His abundant mercy, hath begotten us again to a lively hope by the resurrection of Jesus Christ from the dead, to an inheritance incorruptible, undefiled, that fadeth not away, reserved in heaven for you." (1 Pet. i. 3, 4.) Their security will add much to their happiness.

Now, if it be the fact that heaven is where Christ is, and that where two or three are met together in his name, he is by his Spirit in the midst of them: then you, my brethren, need not imagine that Christ and heaven are a great way from you. Is he not looking in upon us, searching our hearts, carefully noticing the feelings you exercise toward him and his cause?

The more spiritual your views, the nearer Christ will appear to be to you. Have you not, brethren, sometimes found him in the sanctuary, or in the midst of those met together for prayer, or in your closet?

Some of you may soon enter the presence of him who gave his life to redeem you. The remainder of your time on earth which may appear to you long, when it is ended, will appear to be short, and the pleasures of the world but false and deceptive. Think, I pray you, of what has been done for your redemption, and of the returns you have made to your Redeemer. You are now sitting in the outer courts of heaven, my hearers, and the all-piercing eye of Him who suffered on the cross in the room of sinners, is fixed upon you. He offers you, this day, pardon and justification, without money and without price—without any works of your own. The question is now presented to you, Will you accept—will you open your heart and receive Christ as your Saviour or not? Will you even look to Him that you may be saved? His language is, "Come, for all things are ready." Will you come? The prison doors are unlocked, and thrown open; your fetters are knocked off; there is an opportunity for you to make your escape, you are invited and urged to come forth; nothing prevents but your unwillingness. Life and death are before you. I am about to close. Christ is looking upon you, sinner, now under sentence of death; holy angels are witnesses of your decision. Will you not say, Lord, I believe, help mine unbelief! Brethren, we must pray, and pray earnestly, that the Holy Spirit may effect what we cannot accomplish. A great responsibility rests on us. Let us be faithful—leaving to God the results. AMEN.

www.ingramcontent.com/pod-product-compliance
Lightning Source LLC
Chambersburg PA
CBHW070743160426
43192CB00009B/1551